If We're Being Honest

Jennifer Thompson

If We're Being Honest

Urano
publishing

Argentina - Chile - Colombia - Spain
USA - Mexico - Peru - Uruguay

© 2024 by Urano Publishing, an imprint of Urano World USA, Inc

8871 SW 129th Terrace Miami FL 33176 USA

Urano
publishing

Cover art and design by Luis Tinoco

Cover copyright © Urano Publishing, an imprint of Urano World USA, Inc

The first edition of this book was published in April 2024

ISBN: 978-1-953027-40-5

E-ISBN: 978-1-953027-42-9

Printed in Colombia

Library of Cataloging-in-Publication Data

Thompson, Jennifer

1. Parenting & Relationships   2. Motherhood

If We're Being Honest

Table of Contents

HOW WE SEE OUR BODIES

WHO WE ARE

HEALING & HOLDING OUR TRUTHS

Dedication Page

To Jim, for believing in me before I believed in myself.
I love you.

And to my son, Grady, for broadening my world and
restoring my faith. Never doubt the fire within you.

To you, my readers, may you see the fierce potential within each of you. I hope these pages awaken your senses of self-discovery, peeling back layer by layer until you rise unapologetically into who you were designed to be. Together, we are the torchbearers.

Introduction

Somewhere within each of us, our souls are yearning to be free. Free from the confines and silent boxes society, culture, history, and circumstance have placed us in. Quietly infiltrating every facet of our lives, bleeding into everything we do, and all that we know. They tell us *this is normal*. Embrace it. Accept it. Yet, beneath the exhaustion and overwhelm, we ache for something more —a *new* normal. One we define for ourselves, where peace and acceptance flow abundantly.

What if I told you it exists? What if I told you it was possible to boldly claim your own life without fear? Listen, I don't claim to be an expert. But as your sister and friend, I refuse for my voice to be heard from the margins any longer. I've made it to the other side. I've broken free of the falsehoods that namelessly bound me, attempting to place me in a mold I was never meant to be in. Sure, the journey isn't over, but I can tell you from my experience that what awaits you on the other side is something better than you could ever imagine. A life filled with peace, freedom, and the sweet release of unwanted expectations and weight. You don't have to carry it any longer. This idea that we must silently accept glass ceilings and limitations as our reality is a lie.

Today, we stop hiding. Today, we link arms together in community. And while it's true that no two stories are the same, it's our shared experiences that connect us.

Take what you need here.

I pray my words can be a source of inspiration in your own awakening, and that somehow, by sharing my truth, I hope it gives you strength to embrace yours.

While each chapter dissects a failure, belief, or lie we hold to be true as women, I have broken them down into three main areas that impact us the most: shaping our expectations, how we see our bodies, and who we are. Collectively these areas affect our internal psyche in how we live our day-to-day lives and how we envision our future.

The topics and words within these pages may trigger you. While some are light-hearted, others might stir up dormant emotions including pain, or elicit grief, anger, or even rage. There will be parts that may make you uncomfortable, or possibly make you cry, but know that there is healing in our truth. The only way past it is through it. In order to truly understand and know ourselves we must first fundamentally dismantle and unlearn everything we've come to know thus far. Then, and only then, can we awaken and evolve into our most authentic selves.

Take time as you read through these pages. Use the prompts provided to dive deeper into your own healing journey. There may be chapters you consume within minutes, while others you find not to be a problem for you or simply not applicable to where you are in life. That's okay. No two journeys are the same. What led me to where I am today will look drastically different for you.

However, this is my story.

While I write from the perspective of a female and mother, I understand and acknowledge that we all come from various walks of life; therefore, these words will hit each of you differently. My intention is never to exclude anyone through my words. Regardless of gender, sexual orientation, or race, the threads that unite us weave a tapestry of shared experiences and stories. Each of us, as individuals, are worthy of dignity and respect. These stories are not just mine. They are hers, theirs, and ours to hold collectively together. Here you will find a safe space. One of raw honesty and truth. Here you are loved. You are known. You are held.

May we fearlessly rewrite our narratives together.

Now, let's get to work.

SHAPING OUR EXPECTATIONS

Chapter 1

We're All a Little Flawed

Failure Belief: I could be perfect, if only...

Marie Kondo recently made headline news, but it wasn't for promoting her KonMari methodology of decluttering and organizing your life; it was for her honesty. For years, she's been welcomed into the homes of celebrities and women everywhere through her Netflix series. She's built an entire multi-million-dollar empire and brand around her image of clean, crisp, tidy organization and perfection. A quick Google search will show you products, books, classes, and websites referencing and selling her strategies for organizing and living a life of simplicity. You can even hire one of her consultants. Yet, a few days ago the woman who oozed perfection, the one who seemed to have it all figured out, admitted that with three kids...her home is a mess. Her sustainable system of organization wasn't sustainable. She'd given up on being tidy—for now, anyway. Marie Kondo, the professional organizer, wasn't... perfect. Women everywhere breathed a silent sigh of relief. If her home was allowed to be messy, maybe, just maybe, we could be a little easier on ourselves.

I'll go first. My name is Jenn, and I'm a recovering perfectionist. I want to bring attention to the word "recovering" because it's significant. Letting go of perfection is not something you wake up one day and decide you'll never do again. It's a journey. A slow process of deconstructing everything we've been taught. You see, for me, I need things to be flawless, and when I say "things", I mean anything. My need for perfection bleeds into my writing, work, motherhood, parties, body image, home, organization, and even sports. My husband gets annoyed by my organizational tendencies. I have a basket for everything. Hair care, body, batteries, medicine, dental, cleaning supplies, you name it, it goes happily in its wicker basket; appropriately labeled, of course. According to him, I would have a basket to store my baskets if I could, and he's not necessarily wrong. Organizing is the way I feel in control. When my world spins into chaos, I organize. I strip cabinets bare and place everything into categories, creating visual perfection.

Let's be honest; it's not just about baskets. It's my calendar, my notes, and my need to plan everything in advance. I'm OCD about organizing. It's my crutch, the thing I use to try and obtain perfection. Except, like Marie Kondo, labeling everything and placing it neatly into its respective place doesn't change the fact that life is happening around me.

Heck, just the other day I wandered the house trying to figure out why certain areas smelled like a mildewy sewer. I was sure a toilet had overflowed or something had crawled into our walls and died. I yelled for my husband to see if he could determine the source. Twenty minutes later, he did. It was the newly washed towel draped over my head. Apparently, I had left it in the wash a little too long before switching to the dryer. In my defense, I had washed it three times. Finally, on the fourth round, I said *screw it* and swapped the bad boy over before giving it a good whiff. Needless to say, I had to rewash my hair a few times to get the stench out.

My point is this: you can organize your cabinets and declutter your life. You can iron your clothes and have Pantene commercial-worthy hair, but it's an image. You're creating visual perfection in an attempt to cover up the mess. I get it. No one wants to air out their dirty laundry. No one wants to post to their social media feed that they just yelled at their kids and dialed in late to a conference call, but where's this need to portray a certain image coming from? Who the heck was I trying to impress? Was someone going to come into my home and inspect my cabinets like, "Whelp, her drawers are organized and clearly labeled. She's reached the pinnacle of perfection, folks?" Heck, no. That's just weird. Who is going to look down on you if you don't perform at a level that's completely unattainable?

I'll tell you. No one, not even Marie Kondo herself.

But the thing about perfection is it's not just externally driven. Sure, it can be triggered by the world around us and the image we portray, but it can also be created internally by the expectations we set within ourselves; ones I am all too familiar with.

A few years ago, my husband took me golfing. I love baseball, so naturally, he thought I might enjoy golf. And I do—now. However, the first time, I wanted to chuck my clubs down the fairway like in a scene out of *Happy Gilmore*. Don't get me wrong; I can drive the ball, no problem. But getting that stupid little pink ball to go in its home while choosing between eight other clubs that all are for specific distances was enough to send me over the edge (see hatred for sucking at things above). After making countless divots in the fairway, shanking the ball to the left and right of me, and the seven putts it took once I was on the green, I wanted to quit.

"So how many was that?" my husband asked, writing his score on the card.

"I don't know. I stopped counting after eleven," I chirped back.

"Babe, relax. It's your first time. I know you hate sucking at things, but golf takes patience."

"Yeah, well, we all know I have very little of that, especially when I'm not good at something." The hole was supposed to be done in a par 4. Clearly, I needed to do the same. It didn't matter whether or not this was my first time; anything different than that number meant *not good enough*. There were seventy—and eighty—year—old men doing better than I was for crying out loud. Their golf swing looked like an extension of their arm. I would not accept defeat. I could do this. It turns out golf can't be done well when you're tense and fuming beyond measure. I'm sure the birds were chirping that day, but I didn't hear them. After four holes and six balls lost, never to be seen again in the pond where the goose sat silently judging me, I resorted to driving the cart. If I couldn't do it perfectly, I didn't want to do it at all.

I wish I could tell you these were simply two examples and that I've recovered from my perfectionist tendencies, but it would be a lie. I still struggle to set standards for myself that are actually attainable, but when I started seeing perfectionist tendencies in my son I knew I needed to try harder. Grady is an amazing artist; he has been since he picked up his first crayon. His pictures are elaborate and well-illustrated, but as he got older I quickly realized the joy he gets from creating was fading, and at times manifesting disappointment in its place. His drawings needed to be perfect, and when they weren't, it resulted in tears of frustration. I understood exactly what he was feeling and quite honestly, he may have inadvertently picked it up from me. I operated the same way. Grocery lists, recipe cards, post-it notes, and anything that required being written down needed to be perfect. If not, I would crumple it up and start over. I've even gone so far as to throw away a perfectly good card because I screwed up writing on it. Rather than cross it out, I tossed it in the trash and bought a new one. I realize how ridiculous this all sounds, but this was the level of perfection I drove within myself. I was unable to accept anything less.

"Grady, babe. What's wrong?" I asked as my son wiped away tears.

"I jacked up the Komodo dragon and now I have to start over," he cried.

As I looked at the paper, I struggled to see where the "mistake" actually was.

"Babe, I don't see anything. What do you mean? It looks great. This drawing is awesome!"

"No, it's not. I messed it up. It's right there. Don't you see it?" I strained my eyes, desperately searching for what his tiny fingers were pointing to, and that's when I saw it. A minuscule green smudge about two millimeters long, outside the lines.

His drawing was amazing. He creates at a skill level far above his age, but he couldn't see it. His need for perfection blinded him. The image he manifested in his mind didn't match the result. Can't the same be said for so many of us? Perfection takes on many shapes and sizes. It can infiltrate one area of your life or bleed into all of them, but regardless, perfection is almost always rooted in perception and shame. It's wrapped in this idea that if we aren't perfect, we've somehow failed; therefore, we're unworthy of love and acceptance. But love is not contingent on our output.

Listen, I've been there. I've allowed perfection to dictate whether or not I went for something. It's caused me to quit, doubt, fester over disappointing others, and even myself. I think, *if only*. If only I can be pretty enough, smart enough, look a certain way, or work at just the right level, I'll make everyone around me happy. I'll be perfect enough that no one will judge or criticize my choices or who I am. But by reaching for perfection we deny our very existence. We hide our essence, trying to fit a mold we were never meant to be in.

Make no mistake: Perfection is a myth. It's not something any of us can obtain. Life is full of mistakes and regrets. It's impossible to make choices that align with everyone around you. How many times have you sacrificed your own decision to appease someone else? We try to be perfect in the eyes of our parents, spouses, children, and even our friends. But what would happen if we opened up? If we honored our truth by saying I'm not perfect, but this is my decision. You won't love it, but it's what's best for me and most aligned with what I value. You can't perfect your way out of criticism, but you can imperfectly accept love as you are.

In her book, *Daring Greatly*, Brené Brown says this about perfection: "Regardless of where we are on this continuum, if we want freedom from perfectionism, we have to make the long journey from 'What will people think?' to 'I am enough.' That journey begins with shame, resilience, self-compassion, and owning our stories. To claim the truths about who we are, where we come from, what we believe, and the imperfect nature of our lives, we have to be willing to give ourselves a break and appreciate the beauty of our cracks or imperfections. To be kinder and gentler with ourselves and each other. To talk to ourselves the same way we'd talk to someone we care about."

She's right. When I began examining perfection, I found that it's linked to so many other failure beliefs we tell ourselves. It manifests itself in comparison, self-doubt, guilt, expectations, people-pleasing, body image, and even our own qualifications. Listen, if we are truly driven to live a life of authenticity, we have to start by accepting our imperfect nature. It's going to require us to become comfortable with our own stories, talents, and skin. It's going to take us being driven by *our* values, instead of those of the world around us.

"Sweetie, I know you want it to be perfect, but can I tell you a secret?" I said, kneeling close. "Perfect is boring."

"It is?" my son asked, looking confused.

"You bet. If everyone and everything were perfect, how could you ever be you? All of your friends would be the same, and that's not fun, is it?"

"No way!" he exclaimed. "But how do I fix it?"

"You turn it into a happy mistake. Make that little smudge his spikey back. Komodo dragons aren't smooth anyway. Make it unique, bug, just like you."

Quite honestly, I was shocked by my answer, but motherhood stripped away my need for perfection. It exposed my flaws in every way possible. It pointed a finger directly in my face and said, "I dare you." I dare you to tackle it all, and maintain perfection. And, believe me, I tried; for a little while. I attempted to do all the things and do every one of them flawlessly, and it left me in nothing but a puddle of tears. But I had a choice: I could strive for something that didn't even bring me joy, or I could learn to let go. So, I walked perfection to the door and sent her on her way. I was done; done trying to obtain the unattainable. I simply wanted to be myself. I didn't want to hide anymore. I didn't want to worry about who I was or wasn't disappointing, and I wanted my son to see the same.

A few minutes later, he was back in the kitchen, proudly displaying his "happy mistake."

"I like him better when he's not perfect!" he said with a smile. Me too, bug, me too.

~~~~~~

MOVING FORWARD

Do you find yourself struggling with perfection? Identify the areas that drive these tendencies the most.

Are the areas you identified externally driven or are they manifested internally by your own expectations? Remember, high expectations aren't always a bad thing, but how do we keep them outside the realm of perfection?

Where does the need for perfection stem from? What are you afraid of? (i.e.: judgment, disappointing someone, insecurity, failure, love, etc.?)

~~~~~~

Chapter 2

Running on Empty

Failure Belief: I shouldn't need to fill up

Since I got my driver's license I've been on time for everything. Work, parties, family events, coffee with friends, you name it… always prompt. I'm that annoying person who shows up fifteen minutes early, only to stalkily sit in your driveway until the clock strikes a more reasonable time. You know, more like five minutes before said party time. I thrive on routine. Always up at the same time, 5:15 a.m. every morning to start the workday. And then motherhood happened. Like a car crash you can't look away from, it wrecked every ounce of routine I had.

The other day I was running late per usual when my low fuel light came on. *FML! I knew I was going to forget this morning.* On the way home last night I had told myself to remember to get gas on the way to work and now look. I didn't have time for this crap. Didn't the universe know I was running late and short on time? The last thing I needed to do was take ten minutes to pump freaking gas! As I mumbled under my breath, my son's voice came from the backseat, "What's wrong, Mommy?" I glanced back in the rearview mirror, soaking in his innocent little face. He was only three, but he knew enough to know I was stressed.

"Nothing, honey." I sighed. "Mommy is just running late per usual."

His little feet began bobbing up and down as he tried desperately to reach my center console.

"You be a hot mess, Mommy." He giggled, flashing me a toothy grin. He was right. I was a hot mess. I never used to be this way. I used to be on time and organized. Now I was perpetually late and sweating like a woman going through menopause. *My lord, why was it so hot in this car?!*

I whipped into daycare and squeezed into the nearest parking space. The woman parked next to me grabbed hold of her child as if I were some kind of deranged lunatic. "Okay, bug. We've got to hurry," I said clapping my hands like a coach. "Let's move! Let's move!"

As I unbuckled him from his car seat, he laughed. I have a flare for the dramatic, and my son knows my antics well. While I was playfully kidding, I was also equal parts dead serious. I slung him onto my hip, flung his backpack over the opposite shoulder, and headed inside.

"Friends, look who's here!" his teacher shouted over the kids. "Can we give a nice, big hello to our friend?"

"HIIIIIIII!!" they all shouted.

"Okay, baby, have a good day today!" I said, hanging his backpack inside his cubby. "I love you, sweetheart. Mommy will be back to pick you up later today, okay?" I gave him a hug and kiss to get both him and me through the day and walked him over to the breakfast table. As I slipped out the door, I glanced through the window. *I hate mornings like this. When am I going to get it together? OMG, Jenn! Gas. You need GAS!* As I glanced at the clock behind the front desk, I quickly checked on my son while giving the assistant a look of desperation.

"Have a great day!" I yelled as I shuffled out the door.

Tell me I'm not the only mom like this, I thought to myself. When I got in my Jeep, I checked to see how many miles I had left on reserve. Twenty-five. *Okay, as long I take the highway and don't run into any traffic, I should be able to make it.* Logical? Yes. Practical? Hardly. In hindsight, I realize I should have stopped for gas, but we all know any sensible woman in her right mind tests the limits in this case. So, I took my chances. I gambled and ran the bad boy bone dry. I limped it along and...ran into traffic because, of course. I watched the mileage meter tick down as my rage level went up. *For the love, people. Just drive! Move out of the left-hand lane! You've GOT to be kidding me? Another freaking red light?!*

As I entered the security gate, my mileage light dinged again. One mile remaining. Perfect. The nearest gas station was over the bridge about three miles away. A portion of that is downhill, so surely I can make it. I grabbed the only parking spot left in the lot and glanced at the clock—8:51 a.m. *Are you kidding me? I ignored every sign my car was on empty because I didn't have time to fill up and I was still late. I didn't even get gas. How is that even possible?* Blame it on traffic or lack of planning, but whatever the reason, it got me thinking. How often do we do the same?

How often do we rush from place to place, chauffeuring kids like it's our job, filling up our calendars with appointments and parties? We field conference calls in the parking lot at our kid's practice while family dinners look more like drive-thru in the SUV. Our work-life balance is non-existent, yet we lie to ourselves and tell others, "We're just in a season of busy right now." But are we? Will it truly settle down in time? Because, quite frankly, I don't believe it will. We live in a society that glorifies hustle and busyness. Especially from mothers. Women have learned the role of martyr and we play it well. There's something altruistic about being over-committed. Everywhere we turn we hear the word *more*.

Give more. Do more. Be more.

And so, we trudge forward even when every bone in our body is telling us to stop, refuel, and slow down. We push the limits and ignore the signs. We limp along and coast on fumes until there's nothing left.

There was a quote that went viral a few years ago that said, "Women are supposed to work like we don't have children & mother like we don't have a job." It resonated with so many of us for a reason. One sentence had the ability to summarize the load we carry. We live in a society that is hyper-focused on our output. If we're not hustling, then we're not thriving. If we're not manifesting, then we're not living to our fullest potential. We push our bodies to the brink without asking why. What am I actually gaining through the sacrifices made for the sake of the output? I'll tell you. Nothing. I've adopted this set of ideals and standards that aren't even my own. I'm upholding values I don't even align with simply because society tells me I should.

This narrative that we should be doing it all is slowly killing us. I'm sorry, but I'm already running on empty. I'm not going to wake up at 3:00 a.m. to meditate, journal my thoughts on gratitude, and get in a solid one-hour workout. Working out at that hour wouldn't even be effective, anyway. I'm more apt to cause injury to myself or fall back asleep while in the lotus position.

It's not sustainable. We're each given twenty-four hours in a day and I refuse to give up the seven hours I have remaining for sleep to hustle more. I'm tired of letting the world standards be the driver in my life. Somewhere along the way, I formed this perfect image of what motherhood and life would be like, but it's not reality. The reality is, life is messy.

The age-old saying, "You can't pour from an empty cup" is a lie. You can. You can still tip the cup over and pretend to pour. Sure, the cup may be bone dry, but the act of pouring doesn't stop unless you do. You get to choose.

Stop avoiding what's staring you right in the face. Your light is on. It has been for weeks, maybe even months, or years if we're being completely honest with ourselves. You're still pouring, but nothing is coming out. The burnout you feel and anxiety you can't seem to shake are because you're taking on too much. You're overburdened and overworked. It's okay to slow down. It's okay to prioritize yourself in the mix. It's not selfish—it's absolutely essential.

I know not everyone is afforded the luxury of sloughing off our burdens and dedicating countless hours for self-care. But that's not what this is about. Sure, there may be times in our lives when it's possible, but more often than not it's simply not feasible. There are bills to pay and family to care for. The point is, somewhere along the way we've bought into this idea that in order to be a good mom we have to be busy 24/7, or somehow, we're failing. It's a crock.

Do you want to know how to show up best for your family? Start showing up for yourself. It's okay to start small. Check-in with yourself. Is your light on? Pause. Relax your shoulders and unclench your jaw. Take in a deep breath and reset. It doesn't take much. Jam your favorite song, or read a few pages in an inspirational book. Get outside and move your body. Let the sun hit your face (with sunscreen, of course), and breathe in the fresh air. Don't underestimate the power of nature. Disconnect from technology. I know mindlessly scrolling through social media or the news feels like a way to destress, but it's a temporary distraction. It's impossible to reconnect with ourselves when we're stuck in the hamster wheel of comparison or reading about the latest stressors in the world. Trust me, put the phone down.

Some days it will feel next to impossible to squeeze in time for yourself, but do it anyway. The demands of life don't drive your purpose; you do. Do one simple thing for yourself every single day. Don't ignore your light. It's telling you to fill up, and when you do, I promise you'll feel better for it.

~~~~~~~~~~~~~~~~~~~~~~~~~~~~~~~~~~

MOVING FORWARD

Perform an energy scan of yourself. Pay attention to how you feel mentally, physically, and emotionally. How are each of those energy levels? Are there areas where you need to fill up?

List out the things and commitments that drain you, as well as those areas that bring you joy.

Once you've identified the things that fill your cup mentally, physically, and emotionally, schedule time throughout the week to ensure your bucket is being filled.

What are your symptoms of how you feel when you're running on empty? (i.e., easily agitated, resentful, tired, anxious, etc.) Knowing your body's outward response to needing to fill up is half the battle. Take note of what your body is trying to tell you.

When was the last time you checked in with yourself and recharged?

How can you be intentional each day about reconnecting with your-self and doing one thing that energizes you?

Create a zone just for you. This is a safe spot or corner of your home dedicated only to you. The intent is to practice going to this space to recharge and find inspiration.

~~~~~~~~~~~~~~~~~~~~~~~~~~~~~~~~~~~~~~~

Chapter 3

Sitting Still...in Stillness

Failure Belief: I need to be doing all the things

I got sucked up by the vacuum. I wish I were joking, but it turns out all those times your mom told you as a kid that the vacuum can't suck you up, well...it's lies. ALL lies. I can't even tell you how it happened. One minute I'm vacuuming, marveling at my productivity; the next, my foot is halfway in the Electrolux beater while I pray the emergency shutoff kicks in before my entire foot gets wrapped inside. Like, for the love. How does this happen? I didn't know it was possible for your foot to even fit inside. Only I could somehow figure out it is.

I'm happy to say that the emergency shutoff did, in fact, function properly; although not fast enough for the liking of my big toe. After wrangling my foot out and assessing the damage, I hobbled calmly to my little guy, who was playing down the hall. "I need you to go downstairs and tell Daddy to come up here right away."

"Why, Mommy, what's wrong?" he asked.

"I hurt my foot with the vacuum cleaner and I can't really walk. Just go get Daddy."

I would have paid money to see my husband's face in that moment. "Daddy," my son called out on his way to the basement. "You need to get out of your meeting. Mommy got sucked up by the vacuum cleaner."

"Okay, bud. That's great, but I'm a little busy right now," my husband said, assuming it was one of our kiddo's many ploys to get him to play upstairs.

"No, Daddy. Mommy's foot got sucked up in there. It ate her, and she's bleeding. You got to hurry!"

I sat on the hardwood floor clutching my foot, waiting for my husband to reassure me my toe wasn't broken, or worse, falling off. I'm accident-prone by nature, but this was a whole new level, even for me.

As he and my son approached the top of the stairs, he took one look at me and murmured, "Babe, how in the world?" I could see he was trying to hold back laughter.

"Don't even go there." I fought back tears. "Just tell me it's not broken."

Vacuum = 1

Me = 0

I spent the rest of the day with my foot propped up on the couch, trying to keep my big toe from swelling up like a balloon. Everything I had set out to accomplish that day was left unfinished in an instant. I wanted nothing more than to get up off the couch and finish my to-do list. I know, I know. You're probably thinking, good lord, woman. You just got eaten by a vacuum. Just take a breather. But I'm a doer. I hate sitting. It's not something I do well, nor really take the time to do. Sitting means stillness and rest; honestly, who has time for that? Earlier that day, I had been stressing about deadlines and all the balls I was juggling in the air. Or truthfully, letting fall to the ground. And here I was being forced to slow down and rest. That was seriously more tragic than my injured toe. See why my hubby calls me *drama mama*?

I think many of us can relate to this scenario. Okay, maybe not the getting sucked up into a vacuum part, ahem. That one is for me, and me alone. But somewhere along the way, our perception has shifted. Stillness no longer exists. Instead, we welcome busyness and chaos as if it's necessary and simply our way of life. Our schedules are jam-packed and our to-do lists are lengthy. We feel this constant need to be going and pushing or striving for the next big thing in order to feel like we are doing enough.

I don't know about you, but I've been pushing myself for what feels like a lifetime and it's literally gotten me nowhere. The only things I have to show for it are wrinkles, gray hair, a saggy butt, and anxiety. My husband harps on me regularly to slow down and take a breather once in a while. But who has time for that? Not this girl.

Apparently, it takes getting my foot mauled by a vacuum to get me to sit down for a day. That's pathetic but entirely accurate. Injury or sickness is my body's way of forcing me to rest. Neither are healthy, but isn't that true for many of us? Maybe not the injury part, but when was the last time you took the time to rest? It shouldn't take something nearly catastrophic to get us to find stillness.

Take my husband, for example. He's the master of stillness. Believe me, I'm not envious. It actually drives me absolutely insane and is the result of many unwanted death stares and heavy sighs within his earshot. I'm just not wired that way, but I'm learning to be.

This whole vacuum incident got me thinking. Maybe the vacuum is the metaphor for all of the chaos in our lives. Sure, it's loud and clunky, but it makes us feel as though we are accomplishing something and have our lives together. We see the perfectly carpeted vacuum lines and feel relief for an instant, just like crossing off items on a to-do list. So, we lug it around with us wherever we go, even though our backs are tired and we could use a rest. But if we aren't careful, the very things we use to supposedly minimize the chaos within our lives can actually suck us up when we aren't looking. Sometimes it's a slow erode, whereas other times, it's like ripping off a Band-Aid.

I know because it happened to me. Literally. Instead of enjoying stillness and allowing myself the opportunity to recharge, I denied it at every turn. But as I type this, I'd like to think I'm getting better. My foot is, as well. I'm happy to report my toe isn't broken, only bruised. Life has a funny way of getting our attention. Sometimes it takes getting beat up or knocked down (or getting mangled by a vacuum!) to recognize the very thing staring you right in the face. Stillness is okay; in fact, it's necessary.

In an article written for *PsychCentral*, psychologist and clinical director, Karin Lawson, had this to say about stillness:

> Stillness is powerful. Being still is like replenishing the stores. It allows us time and space. It gives us room to self-reflect and actually hear our thoughts. It also soothes our nervous system. Stillness produces the anti-stress fix by allowing us some downtime without totally checking out and being numb to our experiences.

So how do we get there? What kind of practices can we put into place to better quiet the noise around us? Lawson recommends the following (my commentary is added):

1. Remember to breathe – My husband tells me this all the time when I am stressed. He'll stop whatever he's doing, put both hands on my shoulders, look me dead in the eye, and demand I breathe with him. Big breath in, deep breath out. As much as I hate doing it, breathing really does release tension. It slows our heart rate and demands our bodies refocus.

2. Practice when you need it – When we are stressed and overwhelmed, it's easy to think doing more will help lessen our tension, but sitting still while reading a few pages of a good book or listening to our favorite podcast for even a few short minutes can replenish us for the day.

3. Schedule stillness – If you're like me, practicing stillness is hard. If you find yourself struggling to incorporate little pockets of quiet into your day, you may have to be more intentional by carving out specific times. I've become better at doing this both in the evening and at the start of my day.

Blocking time for quiet allows me to start the day on the right foot.

4. Find a favorite spot – Of course, stillness can be done anywhere, but most of us have a place that instantly calms us. Maybe it's your sunroom, back patio, the lake, or a secret walking trail only you know about. Whatever it is, this is your safe place. A space for you to go to bask in the quiet.

5. Listen to soft music – If music were medicine it would be my drug of choice. While I enjoy silence, music is therapy for my soul. It has the ability to make me happy, energize me, and even provide a sense of calm. For me, the violin and piano paired together, Native flute music, or quiet worship songs are perfect when reaching for stillness and calm.

Five simple steps to help us attain peace. Listen, I know what it's like to think the anxiety will lessen and the stress will go away if only we could hustle a little more and get more accomplished. But I'm telling you, it's not worth it. Just because the world is in a constant state of chaos doesn't mean chaos has to reside within you. Those migraines, that pinched nerve, that weight gain, or chronic fatigue you can't seem to shake? It's your body telling you something. Friend, we were never meant to go at this pace. Your body is crying out for intentional rest. Are you listening, or are you like me and just pushing through?

Today I was forced to slow down. I curled up on the couch and snuggled with my little man while watching *The Sandlot*. With my foot propped up high with pillows, my big toe throbbing, I noticed something: I had no agenda. I wasn't multi-tasking. I wasn't staring at my phone. I was simply being in the moment. Sure, the TV was on, but I was sitting in stillness. And you know what? For the first time in a long time I was okay with things being undone.

I guess the secret to happiness isn't found in hustle after all... it's found in stillness.

~~~~~~~~~~~~~~~~~~~~~~~~~~~~~~~~~~~~~~

MOVING FORWARD

As women, we constantly seek to minimize the chaos in our lives, but sometimes the very things we put into place are the things that interfere with our peace. What is getting in the way of you finding stillness?

Is there any part of yourself that feels unworthy if you're not doing?

In what ways can you be intentional each day about reconnecting with yourself and doing one thing that energizes you?

Practice finding stillness each day. Start small. Take one to two minutes, play your favorite song, or take a few deep breaths, and allow yourself space to reconnect with yourself and reset. Create a zone in your home just for you. It can be a room or a corner. The intent is to practice going to this space to recharge and find inspiration.

~~~~~~~~~~~~~~~~~~~~~~~~~~~~~~~~~~~~~~

Chapter 4

Over It

Failure Belief: I should be loving every minute

Potty training nearly broke me. The irony of it all is that I thought it would be a breeze. I mean, how hard could it possibly be to get a three-year-old to poop in a potty? Am I right? *Wrong.* It's laughable, really. The sheer naiveness of it all. I was about to bow down to the porcelain God, and not in the way most of us do in our college days. No. This time the porcelain throne was the enemy. A hole equipped with enough fury to unleash holy terror.

"Bug, do you have to go potty?" I asked my son as he went to his favorite pooping spot behind the chaise of our couch.

"Nooooo!" he argued while veins popped out of his forehead as he pushed.

He was pooping. I knew it. He knew it. Game on.

I picked him up as he thrashed around like I was about to murder him.

"No do it, Mommy!! I not have to go!!!" he yelled.

I set him on the potty, where his little butt cheeks quickly clenched shut and refused to do what nature intended. *Sweet mother, why does this child have to be so stubborn?* He could pee in the potty, no problem. Sure, I may have bribed him with Skittles each time he did the job, but it worked. Number two was proving to be a whole different ballgame.

"Bug, go potty."

"No," he demanded, crying through tears.

"Do you want Mommy to read you a book while you sit there?" He nodded.

There. A truce. Some sense of calm. Thank you! I read the story, hoping to hear a little plop in the toilet, to no avail. We had been at this for over two weeks. He was tired. I was tired.

I was over it in every sense of the word. Yes, motherhood is wonderful, but this was not one of those moments that made me swoon. All of those people who tell you, "Enjoy every moment. It goes so fast." Where were they now? Huh? Crammed in the world's smallest half-size bathroom, I was trying to hang on to my last nerve. This was complete crap. Literally. How something so simple could be this terrifying was beyond me.

"I done," he said, smiling after I finished the last page.

"Absolutely not. I know you have to go. We are not putting on a Pull-Up and going in our pants. No more. We go poop on the potty today!" I was officially declaring mommy law.

"NO! I no like it!" he said, crying through sobs.

"I don't care. There is nothing scary about going in the big boy potty. It's actually easier, bug. Just do it. Relax your bottom."

"Noooooo!! I can't."

It was a battle of wills. Unfortunately for him, he was the product of his mother and he was about to find out just how stubborn I could be. We had one week to master this pooping thing before he transitioned to his new daycare class. I wasn't backing down. It was now or never.

"DO IT, bug! I mean it." I reached for my phone to pull out *Mickey Mouse Clubhouse*. I frantically searched for his favorite one on YouTube with the stupid farm I hated. We had seen the episode a thousand times, but I knew it would calm him down. I hit play. A silence fell over the bathroom, then laughter with a simultaneous PLOP.

"You did it, bug!!" I screamed at the top of my lungs. "You went poop in the potty!! Mommy is so proud of you!"

In shock that he actually did it and the toilet didn't swallow his baby butt cheeks whole, he began to cry. And so did I. Never in my wildest dreams did I think there would come a day I would be so overjoyed about poop that it would render me emotionally unable to contain my tears. But here we were. Wiping butts and tears. Hugging and embracing. High-fiving and happy dancing over the porcelain throne.

That's motherhood in a nutshell. One minute you're about to lose your ever-loving mind, and the next, you're celebrating poop. And still, we don't talk about it. We hide behind perfect Instagram feeds and color-coordinated family photos on Christmas cards. While on the inside, we question every decision we make and worry we're failing our kids. We lock ourselves in the bathroom as little hands peek out from under the door. We cry in our cars on the way to grocery store pickup because we just yelled at our kids and now feel guilty.

Our minds are in a constant battle of real vs. ideal. We set expectations, anticipating them to become our reality, and when they don't, we're left feeling disappointed, frustrated, guilty, or unhappy. We wonder, are we a bad mom for not loving every minute of motherhood? Should we be happier and more grateful than we are right now?

A friend of mine wrote a post that went viral. It was about getting in her car and driving away from her family. She had hit a wall, so she grabbed her keys and left it all right there in the living room. Her husband, the kids, the toys, the mess—all of it. Except she didn't really run away. She found herself in the Sonic drive-thru ordering a cherry vanilla Coke, sucking down her feelings and burying her emotions. She was frustrated, angry, and defeated.

"Good doesn't always equal easy," she says. I honestly don't think I've ever resonated with something more.

This false idealization we've placed on women and mothers is overburdening. We're drowning in #blessed, wondering why the very things we love sometimes drive us crazy and send us over the edge.

But motherhood is hard. Marriage is hard. Work is hard. Being a woman is hard.

Life is hard.

Saying those words out loud doesn't make you less grateful; they make you human. It's okay if today you're over it. I was, too. Motherhood isn't made up of one moment where you lose your cool and yell at the kids. It's made up of a thousand tiny moments pieced together to create the life you love.

You're not failing; sometimes it's just that hard.

～～～～～～～～～～～～～～～～～～～～～

MOVING FORWARD

We've all heard the phrase "enjoy every minute of motherhood." How did it make you feel?

Speaking our truth and giving words to the things that seem hard isn't weak. It makes us powerful. Write down the last time you felt over it.

How can you help the next woman? What phrases can we offer up as encouragement when we are feeling defeated?

～～～～～～～～～～～～～～～～～～～～～

Chapter 5

The Yo-Yo Effect

Failure Belief: I'm never going to be consistent

I did it again. I silently declared this would be the week I got my life together. You know, work out, meal plan, eat healthier, clean the house more consistently, implement a stricter bedtime routine, and of course, drink more water. But as life would have it, all plans were derailed.

Full disclosure: last night's bedtime was an utter disaster. There was no routine, only tears, and an impatient mother. So, if you are one of those peaceful parenting moms whose child has slept blissfully through the night since they were a mere five days old, please don't come at me with your sleep training and parenting skills. I try, okay. Some days are good. Others are a complete trainwreck.

At the start of the school year I was nailing it, packing lunches the night before, setting out cereal bowls, and writing love notes. Lunch boxes were lined up, and I even set my bowl, spoon, and packet of oatmeal out on the (you guessed it) clean counter.

My friend and I had been scouring the internet and plotting how to implement the best school routine and pack ultimate cold lunches.

"I bought a bin for each of the kids' rooms and laminated a chore chart," my friend texted. "Hopefully, it will help make mornings run a little more smoothly."

"Love it! I did something similar. I even bought some cute smiley stickers."

"Let me show you this fun lunch idea I saw on Pinterest," she replied.

I'm pretty confident every food group was adequately represented. Perfectly cut-out fruit shapes of stars and hearts, a little side of ranch for vegetable dipping purposes, and googly eyes donned their sandwiches.

"That's so extra," I responded with a laughing emoji. "Please tell me you're not actually going to attempt that."

But she did, and so did I. Okay, maybe not the perfectly cut-out fruit shapes. No one has time for that, but I did buy adorable lunch box notes to write on every day.

I bet you can guess how long all that lasted…two weeks. Tops.

This morning was anything but organized. Instead of waking up at 6:05 a.m., I woke up an hour later after hitting snooze three times. As I went downstairs half asleep, I threw my hair in a top knot to whip up the lunch I failed to make the night before. My son's Bento box wasn't on the counter. There was no love note or bowls ready for the day. Instead, I opened our half-barren refrigerator (because meal planning is going well) and grabbed an *Uncrustable*, apple sauce pouch, fruit snacks, and chips. Clearly, this was the stuff of Pinterest dreams. Or maybe it was more like Pinterest nightmares.

"It's 7:30!!" I yelled from the kitchen. "Time to get up! You've got 30 minutes before we need to be out the door."

Five minutes prior I was curled up in his bed, kissing his cheeks, telling him how much I loved him. Now I was downstairs yelling like a deranged lunatic.

As I shuffled around the mess to prepare everything for the day, all of my inconsistencies stared back at me. The house looked like a trainwreck. There were dishes piled high in the sink, school papers scattered on the table that my six-year-old refused to part with, along with dried milk stains and crumbs on the counter. I have a dining room table that can't even be used because there is so much random stuff piled on it and the upstairs isn't much better either. Our bathroom looks like complete garbage. As we speak, I have clothes piled up in the corner of my floor. There is fuzzy stuff that will remain anonymous growing in my toilets, and hairspray stuck to my counters.

Do you know what I had for breakfast? Oatmeal, followed by six *Great Value* Thin Mint cookies I managed to shove in my mouth before racing out the door. Completely unnecessary, yes, but also delicious. For a mere $1.87, you too can have a little piece of heaven, although I should preface that these cookies are not your friend. They are the devil reincarnated.

As I shoved the last one in my mouth, reaching for the door, I could hear myself asking *when...*

When are you going to figure out a routine that actually works?

When are you going to lose the weight?

When are you going to be more consistent?

When are you going to get your life together?

The truth is, I can't blame it on motherhood. I've been like this for decades. In my twenties I was a fitness fanatic. I ran all the time. Who am I kidding? It was more like a jog, except you could walk next to me at a brisk pace and keep up. Anyway, I thought it would be cool to say I ran a half marathon, so I signed up with a friend for one up in Chicago. I paid the entry fee and signed the waiver. The only thing left to do was train. I found a thirty-day half marathon running schedule online and printed it off. Do you know how many days I stuck with it? Three. And then—I quit. The thought of failing or coming in dead last terrified me. I never told a soul I signed up for it. The only person who knew was my friend, Rach, and myself. Typing this feels embarrassing. Talk about a complete waste of money. My friend didn't run that half marathon either, but she did go on to run tons of others. She made a promise to herself, committed to running, and nailed it.

Unfortunately for me, I'm a repeat offender. A serial yo-yo'er. I don't know that I'll ever be consistent. Maybe I lack discipline. Maybe I'm doomed to go up and down the same ten pounds for the rest of my life, but whatever it is, I stop and start everything. The one person I fail to show up for over and over again is myself.

Just a few months ago, I signed up for a four-week workout program. I paid $130 for the meal plans, graphs, printouts, and early access. I stuck with it. For four weeks, I checked off the days one by one. The program required me to cut sugar, an act I subsequently thought I might die from. It turns out your coffee doesn't have to look like milk in order to drink it. You can, in fact, drink it black. By drinking it this way, you also unintentionally limit the number of cups you drink a day because, let's be honest, straight black coffee tastes like garbage. The first few days were rough, really rough. I was irritable. I had headaches and I wanted to rage eat an entire row of Oreos, but I refrained. Instead, I begrudgingly measured my portions and ate more greens than I humanly thought possible. After the first week I started to feel better, and by the second week, I started seeing real results.

I completed the four-week program, where I happily lost ten pounds and five inches. I was committed to keeping this healthy lifestyle and limiting my sugar intake. Unfortunately for me, my son's birthday was a few days after the program. I don't know about you, but my love for chocolate store-bought sheet cake with whipped frosting runs deep. I know I swore off sugars and committed to eating better, but you bet your tight yoga pants I was going to devour a quarter of that cake with zero remorse. Surely, one cheat day wasn't going to kill anyone.

The problem was, it wasn't just one day. That cheat day turned into two, then three, and by the time I knew it, I had completely fallen off the bandwagon, again. This is what I do. It's not just one area of my life. It's all of it. I lack patience when I should have it. I'm an organizer who is somehow unorganized. I'm a perpetual planner, yet always late. I drink coffee when I should be drinking water. I order a salad, along with a side of fries. I serve up chicken nuggets on the regular with organic yogurt for good measure. I work out for five days straight and then take a week off (because life). I lose five pounds, only to turn around and gain ten.

I sent a text to my friend after I got home from school drop-off. "I genuinely don't know how to get my life together."

"Same. I can't do it. I feel like I'm constantly failing," she said.

"So, what do we do? I mean, I know what we need to do, and I do it for a few days, sometimes even a week, but then life happens. Someone comes home sick, there are deadlines at work, or kids need to be shuffled to practice and things start falling off my plate. I keep saying today is the day, but it never happens. I don't know how to make it stick. Maybe I just lack discipline. I don't know. Whatever it is, I feel like I'm doomed to repeat this cycle until the day I die."

As I type this, we've embarked on a new year. The calendar has been flipped over and we find ourselves free to dream and start fresh. Like everyone, I have big goals for this year.

1. Lose 40 pounds
2. Save $10,000
3. Complete the manuscript for my book
4. Travel more and be present

But I'm approaching things differently. I'm shifting my focus from the outcome to the progress. Let's be honest; as much as I would love it, forty pounds isn't going to fall off overnight. It's going to take work and time, lots of it. This is where my thinking was always off. I was so fixated on the results. I wanted to lose weight, save money, land a job, learn something new, and when it didn't happen quickly enough or on my timeline—I quit.

Have you been there? Listen, you don't have to accept that the only thing you're consistent at is being inconsistent. Leadership expert and author, John Maxwell, says, "Small disciplines repeated with consistency every day, lead to great achievements gained slowly over time." He's right. I wanted to hang up this writing thing so many times. I got in my head, doubted myself, and questioned how anyone would want to read a book I wrote. I cried. I sat and stared at my screen blankly as no words would formulate in my brain, but word by word, sentence by sentence, I showed up. I did it, and you can too.

Oftentimes, when we hear about people's journeys or read their success stories, what do we see? The before and after photos. The side-by-side comparison of someone miserable and overweight next to the slim, sculpted new version. We read about the in-debt college student who invested five thousand dollars in a business venture, only to turn it into a Fortune 500 company. Everywhere we look, we're flooded with images of before and after. We think, I want that, but what they fail to show you is the messy middle. The hard parts of the journey, where they wanted to quit but pushed through. Instead, we see the results of an eight-week workout program where someone lost thirty-seven pounds and looks like a whole new person, but their journey is in the details. The sacrifices they made. The level of commitment they showed, and the makeup of their bodies. Our results were never meant to be a one-size-fits-all. What works for one person may not work for you. That doesn't mean you've failed. It means you have your own path.

This year, I'm focusing on the small wins. I'm embracing the journey rather than the destination. I'm giving myself grace in knowing that while each day may be different, my commitment to myself stays true. While the path may not always be straight, I can show up. I can try because each day I continue forward, I move one step closer to my end goal.

I wrote down a list of twelve wins this year, each feeding into my four bigger goals. I like to call them progress wins. Milestones on the journey to the end goal. I bought some craft bags, along with tags to go on the outside (because cuteness is a priority), a few mini bottles of champagne, and some gift cards. On each tag, I wrote a progress win and placed one of the items inside. As I reach each small win, I'll open the bag and celebrate. Maybe that's with a little bubbly or a coffee at Starbucks, but whatever it is, it's worth taking a moment to acknowledge my progress.

That's where we trip up. A new year comes along, and we're motivated to change, but motivation is temporary. Sure, it has its purpose and helps us get started, but discipline and consistency are what will get you to your destination.

You don't have to accept that the only thing you're consistent at is being inconsistent. You simply need to start small. Identify one or two things you'd like to change and focus your efforts there, but within reason. For example, if you want to start working out five days a week, but work full-time, with a one-hour commute each way, plus have kids in extra-curricular activities halfway across town three of those five days, maybe just commit to two days a week. The times I quit, I focused on too much, all at once. You can't cut sugars, dairy, or gluten, and vow to only eat salad and protein, while simultaneously working out seven days a week for two hours straight. I mean, you can, but how sustainable is that?

Recognize that consistency is a habit formed. According to a 2021 study performed by *The British Psychology Society*, it takes a minimum of 59 days to reach peak habit formation. In other words, this isn't something that will happen overnight, and it won't always be perfect. The point is you continually move forward and do the work. Rather than focusing on the quality of your consistency, understand that on any given day different variables impact our level of intensity, and how we show up. A day where you have all the free time in the world will most likely result in high levels of output. The next day, you may be lining up barf buckets, praying you don't fall victim to the latest virus your kids brought home. On days like this, your output may be next to nothing. That's okay. It doesn't mean you're inconsistent. It means life happened. Pull your bootstraps up and get back on track when you can.

Ironically, an episode of *The Mel Robbin's Podcast,* called "5 Essential Hacks I'm Using to Make New Habits Stick," focused on how to become more consistent. Her hacks are so simple, yet I had so many head-nodding moments. I've outlined them below (the added commentary is my own).

Hack #1: Make it visible – This may be the most basic thing on the planet, but she's right. How many times do we set goals for ourselves, like we want to drink more water, exercise daily, and just generally get our life together, but we keep it all in our heads? I'm telling you right now, if I have to pick out my workout clothes at 5:00 a.m. in the morning, I'm not freaking doing it. I prefer the warmth of my bed over standing there half-naked staring into my armoire wondering what in the heck I'm going to wear. I'm wearing pajamas, and I'm going back to bed. Period. When we have goals but need to make twenty-seven decisions before we can even start, we don't stick to them. We lack willpower because we've already set ourselves up for failure. By picking out our clothes the night before and setting the water bottle next to our vitamins, we remind ourselves of our intentions.

Hack #2: Get it Out – Listen, I have a serious sweet tooth. It is my downfall, and I know it, so if my goal is to reduce my sugar intake, does it make sense to have a bunch of cookies, soda, and cream cheese danishes lying around the house? Hell, no. I cannot be trusted. I will be shoving that crap in my face at the counter with zero remorse. My willpower and discipline are simply not that strong. For you, maybe it's not sugar. Maybe instead, you want to cut out dairy, gluten, or alcohol, but whatever it is you're trying to eliminate, take it slow. Remember, eliminating it cold turkey can create unhealthy binging habits later down the road. Instead, find alternatives and options that work for *you.*

Hack #3: Track Your Progress – I'm all about leaving the spreadsheets and graphs for the office, but she's got a point. I've tried to track my progress for years in my head. Do you know how far it's gotten me? A week tops. I never commit or follow through on anything when it's simply a mental goal in my head. Again, this goes back to making it visual. There is something empowering about crossing off each calendar day or watching the circle light up on your fitness watch. You feel accomplished, and you can visualize your progress.

Hack #4: Create a Plan – I don't know about you, but I've tried to make meal planning stick about two hundred times, and do you know why I consistently fail? I don't stick to the plan, or worse, I don't plan at all. I wing it. I have meal ideas (in my head, of course) and then when the day rolls around to make something, I bail and order a pizza. There's nothing to visualize. I didn't think about schedules or timing. I didn't ensure that I had all of the ingredients to even make the freaking meal in the first place, so I phone it in. Literally. We have to stop making excuses and start planning ahead. Look at schedules, take note of the weather if you're planning to work out outside, create a plan, and then have an alternative if something goes awry.

Hack #5: Do it in the morning – I'm not going to lie; this one makes me want to throw up a little. I am a morning person, but I also really, really love sleep. I do, however, realize that the most productive people tend to be those who start their day on the right foot. I'm not going to scream *maximize your time* here on this one. Do what works for you. If getting up 30 minutes before your kids get up is feasible, do it. If you were up five times in the middle of the night, prioritize rest. Find a time that works for you, and plan to accomplish your goals during that time. End of story.

The point of all of this is simple: having intention, making things visual, and creating a plan allow us to set ourselves up for success rather than failure. Unfortunately, too many decisions over time create decision fatigue, which leads to quitting. James Clear, author of *Atomic Habits,* says this about willpower:

> As it turns out, willpower is like a muscle. And similar to the muscles in your body, willpower can get fatigued when you use it over and over again. Every time you make a decision, it's like doing another rep in the gym. Similar to how your muscles get tired at the end of a workout, the strength of your willpower fades as you make more decisions. When your willpower is fading and your brain is tired of making decisions, it's easier just to say no.

By making simple, effective choices, we drive ourselves to make better decisions. When talking with my friend recently about consistency and creating better habits, she said something that clicked in my brain. She had purchased a habit tracker where she outlined areas where she was struggling and built out habits she could practice to help in those areas.

She said, "I'm not joking when I say that seeing it constantly, walking by it every day, has been so motivating. I want to cross it off, and when I don't, I'm mad at myself for breaking the streak. But here's the real ah-ha moment for me. She went on to say, "Before we lay down, I do 'closing duties.' Quickly clean/tidy the house, do the day's dishes, pack kid's lunches, prep coffee for the morning, pack backpacks, and lay out everyone's clothes."

Something about the words "closing duties" registered within my brain. It simplified it and broke it down in a way that felt completely attainable. So, I purchased a habit tracker on Amazon. It's a circle that keeps track of habits month by month, but while I've been waiting for it to ship, I've been starting small and tackling my "closing duties" nightly. The impact those few things have had on my mood before I sleep, as well as how I feel in the morning, is next level.

Ask yourself what is most important to you. What are the areas you find yourself struggling with that you wish to change? Maybe you want to be in better shape, use the gym membership you purchased, travel more, fix your finances, be on time more, build your business, or learn salsa.

Whatever it is, you're not failing. You're not doomed never to be consistent or get your life together. You simply need a plan. Stop focusing on the *when*, and instead see the journey. Remember, some days you will get it right, the stars will align and you will crush every to-do list and goal you set for the day. Others will look like a complete dumpster fire. It's okay. The point is, we continue to move forward. One day at a time. We're all a work in progress. Stop beating yourself up over something you're not. Figure out your why, then write it down and leave it somewhere you can see it every single day. Set the small milestone progress wins along the way, and get after it. Today, we start by celebrating that each day we're one step closer to becoming the best version of ourselves.

MOVING FORWARD

What does consistency mean to you?

Identify where and why you are experiencing inconsistencies. For example, is it coming from a place of fear of failure, or because your priorities are not in alignment with what is important to you?

What areas do you want to grow in or change? Rate them from 1-10 based on priority to help you identify where to focus first.

How can you make time and create a place for it in your daily routine?

When we fail to stay consistent or reach our goals, it's usually because we don't celebrate along the way. How can you break down your goals into incremental progress wins that feel attainable?

Chapter 6

It Can Wait

Failure Belief: I don't have enough time

I recently took an unconventional day off. I needed to get some shopping done for the holidays, so like any sensible woman, I decided to jam-pack my agenda with to-do's along with a quick pedicure (because you know, self-care). For three days, I had deliberated on whether or not I should even attempt it. I didn't really have time. The last thing I wanted to do was sit there for an entire hour, fretting over everything else I should be doing in that time-frame, but it had been three years. My toes needed this. I needed this. I had exactly forty-five minutes before my appointment, just enough time to head into town and maybe grab a Starbucks. Instead, I headed to Kohl's to grab an online pick-up order. Surely, I could run in really quick and then jet across town.

I made my way through the parking lot, finding a spot near the back, and put it in park. The place was packed. I glanced at the clock; thirty-five minutes. *Okay, let's make this quick.* As I grabbed the handle of my car door to head inside, that's when I saw her. An elderly woman, barely five foot tall, with gray hair and a cane. I watched as she took one unsteady step after another, her purse flopping against the cane shaft, making her wobble a bit. She'd pause and pick up the heavy Kohl's bag with her right hand, then set it down and repeat. *Surely someone will stop and help her.*

There were people walking into the store in droves, but as I got closer, no one stopped. A few of them had even walked right past her. I could feel my conscience tugging at me. *Help her. What's the worst she might say? No? At least you offered.* I picked up the pace, and when I got within earshot, I asked her.

"Ma'am, do you want me to carry that for you?"

"Oh goodness, thank you. That would be wonderful," she said, turning around. "Or you can go in and get me a cart."

"Why don't I just carry it for you and walk with you? I want to make sure you get across the crosswalk okay. I'll get you a cart once we get inside."

"Thank you. You know I ordered about fifteen pairs of jeans online just to find the one style that would work for my tiny little legs, and now I have to lug them all back inside to return them. Are you sure you have time to do this?"

"I'm in no hurry. I have all the time in the world," I said, smiling at her.

Five minutes ago, I was racing against the clock, sweating through my coat as I thought about all the places I needed to get to by 2:30 p.m. The truth is, I knew I didn't have time for half of it, but for whatever reason, here I was. *Kohl's* bag in hand, time ticking away, and I couldn't care less. I was right where I needed to be.

"I feel like I should pay you," she said as we got inside.

"No, ma'am. This is just basic humanity." I turned around as I grabbed a cart. "When we see someone in need, we help."

As we parted ways, I couldn't help but smile. I headed to the back of the store to grab my order and then left. I never ran into the woman again. I didn't even catch her name, but it felt good to see another human. To meet them where they were and extend a helping hand. It took what, all of four minutes? I still even managed to make it on time to my appointment.

This whole encounter got me thinking. How often do we utter the words *I don't have time* in a day? Maybe we say it to ourselves, to our kids, our spouses, or even our co-workers. Regardless, we've become tethered to time. Running frantically from one place to another. Racing against the clock. Stretching it. Maximizing it to see just how many hours in a day we can utilize to bleed out the most productivity. We accept that this is simply the way life is because our society shows us no other way, but what if it's the opposite? What if, instead of all this racing, we paused and took a breath?

Think about it. How many people did you come across today? The frazzled and sleep-deprived mom pushing her crying toddler in Target, did you see her? The woman wiping away tears behind you in the Starbucks drive-thru. The man who cut you off in traffic. The elderly gentleman struggling to reach for a can of soup at the grocery store. Did you see them, or were you too busy racing around to notice?

I'm going to be honest, we're missing it every single day. We are seeing people, but we aren't truly *seeing* them. We're missing our own babies and loved ones for the pursuit of things we don't even care about. We tell ourselves, "There just aren't enough hours in the day," as we cry in the shower because we feel like we're failing. Failing to uphold a standard that isn't even our own. Time isn't the problem; our mindset is. Not everything is a necessity. I need you to read that one more time because it's important. *Not everything is a necessity.*

I can't tell you how many times my husband has looked me dead in the eye as I'm going one hundred miles an hour, grumbling about how I don't have time to do x, y, or z, and said, "It can wait. Whatever you're doing, leave it and come [fill in activity with the boys here]." An invitation to live in the moment instead of spinning around in a constant state of *doing*. As much as I may push back, I'm always thankful I listened. Trust me, the dishes don't have to be done this instant. The furniture doesn't have to be dusted on a weekly basis. You don't have to scrub the toilets on the sunniest day of the year. It can wait.

We don't have a time problem; we have a prioritization problem. Trust me, I'm working on being better at it. I don't know about you, but I'm tired of choosing the dishes over my kids. I'm tired of accepting that sleep is simply for when we're dead. I'm tired of sacrificing my humanity in a quest to maximize every waking moment.

I get it. I know we're all busy, but we can't get so busy we forget to enjoy the life right in front of us. Time is sacred. It's one of the most precious gifts you can give someone. When we give of our time, we say to that person, "you matter. I see you." Whatever you're doing, I guarantee you it's not as important as you think it is. It can wait. You can spare five minutes, trust me. Don't fall into the trap of I don't have enough time. I've been there. I watched as all of those people walked right past that elderly woman. I've seen the face of disappointment in my son as I begrudgingly dismissed his request to play because mommy didn't have any time.

We have to start looking up, past the to-do list and daily grind. People are walking around begging to be seen. Put down the phone and close your laptop. Look a stranger in the eye. Tell your child yes, even when every bone in your body says you should be doing. Because here's the thing: in a world where technology has connected us like never before, I'd argue we've never been more disconnected. The emails can wait. Not everything has to be crossed off, except for the one-line item that should be at the very top. The one that reads: "you lived, not for the hours, but for the moments." We didn't race against time; we cherished it. We saw people. Our people. We loved them well, helping random strangers along the way.

~~~~~~~~~~~~~~~~~~~~~~~~~~~~~~~~~~~~~~

MOVING FORWARD

Each of us is given 24 hours in a day. Do you fill yours with never-ending to-do lists and unrealistic expectations, or do you leave room for life?

We must be mindful of the expectations we've adopted. Are they ones you've set, or were they handed down to you by society, or your parents, siblings, job, etc.?

What does it mean to YOU to be in the moment? What does that look like? How do you feel?

~~~~~~

Chapter 7

Sorry, Not Sorry

Failure Belief: I need to apologize

My mom recently stopped by to drop off a few things. "Sorry the house is such a mess," I apologized, opening the door. "I've been meaning to get some cleaning done today, but I've been swamped with work." In all fairness, it had been a day and the state of my home proved it. There were toys all over the living room floor, dried Cheerios stuck to the table from this morning's breakfast, dishes piled high, and laundry draped over the banister in hopes that it might actually make it upstairs.

But it was my home. I didn't have to rationalize or explain anything. Still, for whatever reason, I felt it necessary to apologize to my own mother. I felt embarrassed and ashamed, and for what, simply living? Managing work, life, and kids is messy. It's not meant to be perfect all the time, but still we try.

As women, we apologize for everything, from the way we look to the reason we're late or didn't return a missed phone call. We say we're sorry for the delayed email, as if we did something wrong. We apologize for not being able to be a room mom for the latest kindergarten party, or for not responding in the group chat. We say sorry when someone bumps into *us* or for our child being sick. We apologize for our own parenting choices, for crying out loud.

But not everything requires an explanation. You don't have to rationalize every action or choice you make. Sure, it's important to admit when you're wrong, but apologizing for something that isn't even your fault is crazy.

Think about it. How often do you find yourself apologizing on any given day?

Sorry, this might be a stupid question. I apologize for the delay in getting back to you. Sorry, I need to leave a bit early for a doctor's appointment. I'm sorry to bother you. Can I get a few minutes of your time? Sorry you had to listen to me vent. I'm sorry, can I get a refill on my water?

Just reading those sentences makes me want to throw up. We cushion every decision and action we take with an apology out of fear of being seen as offensive or too assertive. I have literally watched as women apologized simply for taking up space as if somehow our mere existence requires an explanation. This fear of being labeled as *bossy* or viewed in any sort of negative light encourages us to downplay our own successes. For a woman, you can win or succeed, but not without regard for the feelings of others. From the moment we're born, we're conditioned that while we can be confident, we must also be humble. Our individualization is encouraged, but not without stipulations. This constant contradiction and hyper-awareness of how our actions may somehow affect others leaves us over-apologizing to compensate and appease those around us. Sometimes done out of fear, while other times out of mere habit.

Apologizing erodes our value. It's as if we're openly stating we're somehow in the wrong. It diminishes our confidence not just within ourselves but also in how others view us. Saying the words "I'm sorry" or "my apologies" with every statement made or email sent removes all credibility, as if our beliefs, opinions, and voice are a mistake. Apologizing becomes our crutch, a scapegoat, and a sure-fire way to ensure our likeability stays intact, but what we fail to see is the chipping away of our own self-esteem.

I can count on one hand the number of times I have heard my husband apologize. His choices are just that, his. His opinions?

Yep, he stands firm in those too. No statement, view, or choice is peppered with "I apologize" or "I'm sorry." He's simply himself. Take it or leave it. That's not to say that he never apologizes. He simply only apologizes when he feels he's done something wrong. He doesn't apologize for existing or for having an opinion.

I, on the other hand, do. I'm working on getting there, but like everything, it takes time. Time to undo the years of cultural appropriation of what "good girls" are to do and be. Of course, manners are necessary, that's not what we're arguing here, but we have to get beyond this idea that we must be polite first, and bold second. Because that second part never comes. You can't stay true to who you are while trying to fit a mold of what society tells you you should and shouldn't do.

So, how do we elicit change and unknow everything we've been taught? In an article written for *Forbes* magazine, titled "How Women Can Stop Apologizing and Take Their Power Back," Caroline Castrillon identifies three things we can practice right now, to stop apologizing so frequently.

1. Practice self-awareness
2. Change your vocabulary
3. Be confident and intentional

Let's dissect the first one. Self-awareness gets back to my earlier point of being aware of how often we find ourselves apologizing. It's important to note not just the frequency but also the triggers or situations where you tend to do it more. For example, a situation might be you find yourself apologizing in the workplace. Maybe it's the idea of speaking up in meetings or asserting yourself when in a confrontation. When we talk about an individual trigger, this could be a co-worker or a boss who has you on edge or feeling inadequate. It's important to remember, though, that over-apologizing doesn't simply happen within the workplace. You can be triggered by your parents, mother-in-law, or male boss. A neighbor, friend, or even a stranger.

By becoming more self-aware, we can begin to recognize triggers and actively work to change our vocabulary. I know it may seem trivial, but altering a few key phrases or words is one of the most impactful ways we can alter our dialogue. I've been studying this for so long now that I notice every time a female friend or counterpart apologizes. Each time, my heart sinks. Ninety-nine percent of the time, it's completely unwarranted. It's constant, but we have the power to change it. Just the other day, I received a follow-up email nudging me on a response that I was delayed in answering. My initial reaction was to start off by saying, "I'm sorry," but instead I wrote: Appreciate your patience. [followed by the answer]. Such a simple change, but one we as women need to do more of.

I'm going to be honest. As I slowly inch closer to breaking the habit of unwanted apologies, I've become empowered. It turns out that's the natural progression into Step #3. I feel more direct and assertive in my answers. I doubt myself less and initiate more. I'm okay with things being slightly uncomfortable because I accept that it's not my responsibility to always smooth things over. Do I always get it right? No, but with enough practice and self-awareness, we can retrain our way of thinking into one that doesn't shy away from being our authentic selves, but rather who we are, no apologies necessary.

~~~~~~~~~~~~~~~~~~~~~~~~~~~~~~~~~~~

MOVING FORWARD

Take note of how often you find yourself apologizing in a day. Why are you apologizing? What is the feeling you are trying to avoid or overcome by saying you're sorry? Is the apology coming from a place of heartfelt sincerity or out of habit?

Ask yourself, am I apologizing for other people's reactions to my behaviors and choices?

Before you apologize, practice pausing and evaluating the situation to determine if an apology is necessary. In most cases, you will find you can rephrase your response.

Write down a few key phrases you can leverage instead of defaulting to an apology.

~~~~~~

Chapter 8

Toast & Jam

Failure Belief: I shouldn't be burnt out

"Mommy, I need you," my son yelled from his bed. I tapped the screen of my phone charging on the nightstand to see what time it was. 6:35 a.m. on a Saturday.

"Whyyyyy," I moaned as I threw the bed covers off, shuffling to my son's room. Without saying a word, I crawled into bed with him, hoping he would go back to sleep.

"I missed you while I was sleeping," he said, squishing his chubby cheeks in close for a good morning kiss.

"I missed you while I was sleeping, too. Although I wish you would sleep longer."

I wanted more than anything to go back to sleep and hide from all of life's responsibilities, but unfortunately, I knew better. I was up for good.

As I made my way downstairs to brew some coffee, I prayed it would spark something within me and bring me back to life. While I waited for the liquid gold to percolate, I sat lifeless on the couch staring into oblivion.

"Will you color with me?" my son asked.

"Mommy needs a few minutes, babe. Give me a bit to wake up, and then I'll color, okay?"

I felt off. I couldn't tell you what the culprit was or why I felt the way I did, but it wasn't going away. I had been like this for weeks. I tried everything. Water. Coffee. Retail therapy, even meditation, which by the way I don't know that I will ever master, but nothing worked. When I texted my friends to commiserate and see if I was, in fact, the only one failing at life, we all said the same thing—we were tired. But not the kind of tired a good twelve-hour stretch of sleep could fix, or a one-hour session at the nearest spa would remedy. It was bigger—much bigger. We lacked energy and focus. We were walking around like emotionless zombies, numb to our surroundings. Nothing fazed us anymore, not even the latest headlines on the news.

It's no wonder why. This lifestyle of doing it all leaves no margin for self.

And yet, we're handed a bottle of bubble bath and a candle and told to take thirty minutes to practice self-care and decompress. As if somehow that amount of time can erase the fact that women are supported by a system that doesn't support us back. Why else would we be asked to return to the office weeks after giving birth? Or provided a health care system that doesn't work for everyone? Our society was built on a hierarchical system that doesn't thrive when women stand firm and say *enough*. It's dependent on our willingness to serve. Like something hard-coded into our marrow, we believe it is our moral obligation to give without question. It's to provide and nurture those around us, even at the expense of our own well-being. When we fail to keep those around us happy, we feel unworthy. And so begins the vicious cycle of giving, even when our cups are empty. The list between what we love, and what brings us joy and fulfillment, becomes muddied with the responsibilities laid out before us and of everyday life. Our very existence becomes one giant to-do list we're destined never to complete.

Our bodies are no longer our own. We've become enslaved to upholding a value that isn't one we ourselves believe in. Yet, we never stop to question whether what we're doing is truly something we want, or if it's what we've been *taught* to want. Instead, we sit willingly in the passenger seat and allow the world to be the driver in our own lives. We cover up our angst and uncomfortableness that sits deep within our bellies by doing more, instead of getting comfortable with silence. If we listened and paused for even a moment, the silence would tell us this isn't what we want at all. Instead, we've allowed the noise of the world to encompass our thoughts and dictate what we should want and how to get there.

After a few minutes zoning out on the couch, I decided I should probably eat something, so I put a few pieces of toast into the toaster, along with an extra one for my five-year-old. After a few minutes, I could smell something burning. The toast.

As I pulled the blackened slices out of the toaster oven, my son made a barf face.

"I'm not eating that!" he said, running away. "It's burnt!"

"Well, I'm not wasting it. I'll throw some butter and jam on it, and you won't even notice."

"Ew, strawberry jam is gross, Mom. I don't want any. I'll just have some cereal."

The toast looked as burnt as I felt. As I reached for the jam to drown the taste, I had an epiphany. I didn't need to cover it up. I could scrape it off. It was only burnt on the surface from being too close to the warmers. It was excess. I didn't need it.

Friend, the toast was me. I was burnt out from consuming and doing what everyone else told me I should be doing. I knew most of it was unattainable, but instead of scraping it off and protecting my own well-being, I allowed myself to sit there longer. Instead of addressing what was burning me out, I covered it up by adding more crap. I put on a fake smile and pretended all was well. I smeared some jam on it, hoping no one would notice.

Make no mistake, the overwhelming heaviness you feel is brought on by the culture our society promotes. It's the result of placing the needs of everyone and everything before your own. Regardless of how you feel about gender roles and responsibilities, women still largely fulfill the role of caretakers. Add in family issues, finances, work responsibilities, daily commutes, children,

extracurricular activities, caring for elderly parents, grocery planning, and everything in between, and the result is—burnout. What
you are feeling is real. It has a name and characteristics that define
it. I know because I've been there. It's no longer something that
only happens within the workplace. It's happening within our
homes. Burnout is the result of continuous overwhelming stress
on our physiological makeup. It's not the same as depression or
anxiety. Yes, they can overlap, but depression is typically de-
scribed as something that doesn't dissolve even when the stress
has been removed.

So, what are the symptoms? How do we know the difference,
and what can we do about it? According to Emily and Amelia Nagoski, cowriters of the book *Burnout: The Secret to Unlocking the
Stress Cycle,* burnout manifests itself in three primary ways: deper-
sonalization, decreased sense of acknowledgment, and emotional
exhaustion.

For me, emotional exhaustion was the main offender, followed
by fatigue, detachment, and irritability. There was seemingly no
end in sight. I was drowning in my own inability to keep up. The
demands were no longer attainable. Sister summarized it perfectly
in an episode of the *We Can Do Hard Things* podcast when she
said, "Burnout is when every single moment requires something of
you, and there are more requirements than there are moments in a
day."

I felt that. Maybe right now, you're where I was. Maybe you
can't find words to describe how you're feeling, but you know
you're going through the motions. Not living, just existing. But
this isn't how life is supposed to be. You don't have to accept that
fatigue and this never-ending cycle are simply a part of who you
are now. We don't have to go through life burnt out and exhaust-
ed 24/7. It doesn't always have to be go-go-go. It's perfectly acceptable to scrape off the things that cause stress in your life and
trigger you. You're not required to perform miracles simply because others expect it of you. You're not morally obligated to do
any of it.

Start by eliminating some things in your life that you know cause stress. Ask yourself *how can I lighten my load?* Perhaps it's protecting your time and freeing up space on your calendar or creating a routine to accomplish specific tasks throughout the day, including downtime for yourself. Whatever it is, replace those gaps with things that fill you up. Get comfortable asking for help, and for space when you need it. Pay attention to those you spend time with. Make sure it's with individuals who revitalize you and make you feel refreshed. Take inventory of the things you mentally consume, whether it be on the news or in your social media feeds. Is it feeding you or depleting you? And most importantly, honor yourself. Not who society tells you you should be, but who you are at your core. You can take back control.

"Hey, the bread isn't burnt anymore! You fixed it!" my son screeched.

"I sure did," I said, setting down the butter knife. "Now, who's ready to color?"

Turns out you don't have to take on more. You just need to learn how to scrape off what you don't need.

~~~~~~

MOVING FORWARD

Do you believe you may be experiencing burnout? Burnout can manifest itself in many different ways, as outlined above. However, most commonly, it includes irritability, detachment, fatigue, heightened anxiety, difficulty concentrating, etc. Take time to self-evaluate yourself and identify any symptoms you may be experiencing.

Are your schedule, work, life, and daily activities setting you up for success or failure?

If you answered no to the question above, what variables within your day are adding to the stressors and stripping you of joy? Identify them, along with whether or not they can be eliminated altogether.

If your schedule/activities are not the culprits for causing stress in your life, are you creating more by setting unrealistic expectations? Identify what they are.

How can you better ensure your mental and physical health is a priority? List three things that bring you joy, and do more of it.

Chapter 9

Baggage Claim

Failure Belief: I need to be carrying it all

We got my son's diagnosis five months before his third birthday. A year prior, on September 23rd, I first noticed something was wrong. We were in the toy room playing puzzles when he grew seemingly frustrated. As I dumped the pieces out onto the floor to start fresh, his chubby little fingers grabbed for a puzzle piece... and missed. My hands began to shake as panic set in. He had just hit his head a few days ago at daycare. Was something wrong? I placed another puzzle piece in front of him and asked him to put it where it went. His hand reached again a few inches away from where the actual piece lay. Tears set in as his frustration mounted. I reassured him that everything was fine, not believing a single word I was telling him...or myself. I ran to my husband in the other room, hoping I was just panicking over nothing. I didn't know.

"I think something is wrong with Grady. He can't grab his puzzle pieces. I don't think he can see," I said anxiously. As we entered the room, my husband laid his head on the ground to get a clear look at what our son's vision was doing, and that's when we saw it. His left eye was crossed inward. He couldn't grab objects because he was seeing double. As my son lifted his head, his eye stayed inward. It was everything I could do not to burst into tears. I was terrified for my baby.

"What do we do?!" I whispered to my husband, trying to remain as outwardly calm as I could.

"Take a picture and call the doctor, right now."

I sent a text to our pediatrician:

"I'm sorry to bother you, but we've got a bit of an emergency. Grady's eyes are completely crossed, and he keeps missing objects he's reaching for. I don't think he can see."

We scheduled an urgent appointment with the doctor. After a CT scan to check his neurological function, referrals, countless eye exams, testing, and eye therapy, we finally had our answer—strabismus.

Strabismus is doctor terminology for crossed eyes, typically corrected with early eye therapy found in special eyewear or patching to create better alignment. Unfortunately for us, after trying these over the next eight months, neither worked. He would need corrective eye surgery.

We wanted the best surgeon, and the best would take us two and a half hours away to the University of Iowa Stead Family Children's Hospital. The surgery took approximately two hours, during which they cut the interior and exterior muscles of both his eyes. When he came out of anesthesia, his eyes were swollen and bloody. As he came to he began thrashing and screaming. The arm buddies, attached to his little arms and meant to prevent children from touching and rubbing their eyes were sending him into a state of panic.

I cried as my husband and I took turns holding him close to our chest, trying desperately to keep his arms away from his face. As a parent, you would do anything to take away your child's pain. You would switch places with them in a heartbeat.

The next six weeks of recovery were hard and long, but the surgery was effective. Multiple trips to and from Iowa while juggling work was taking its toll. The sleepless nights and worry were affecting us both, however, thankfully his vision improved. It turns out he also has astigmatism. One pair of blue-rimmed glasses later and I have my own little Jerry Maguire kid.

I share this story because haven't we all been there at some point in our lives? Maybe it's not strabismus, but we've all experienced

the toll of carrying extra baggage, whether emotionally or physically. Every single day we encounter people dealing with the unimag-
inable. Maybe it's the loss of a loved one or an unwanted medical
diagnosis. A relapse. A deteriorating friendship or family crisis.
Maybe it's job loss or financial issues. Divorce or heartbreak. And
when we do, we're left feeling one thing—alone.

It's funny how life works. One minute you're running around
complaining about how full your calendar is and how much you
need a break, and then bam! Something unexpected happens, and
you find yourself asking why? Why me? Why now? And more importantly, how will I ever get through this?

When I was dealing with my son's diagnosis, I was also struggling with postpartum depression and anxiety. I was emotionally
and physically drained, yet no one could see the extra baggage I
was carrying around every single day, except my husband and
Mom. I put on my makeup and hid the pain behind my smile.

The load was invisible, but still just as heavy. Maybe even
more so.

Internationally acclaimed nutritional biochemist, Dr. Libby
Weaver, describes the invisible load as, "the stress we carry that no
one sees, that drives how we think and feel. From the physical load
on our body to the emotional load in our mind, this invisible load
is what really sits at the heart of our stress."

Hang with me for a sec while I break this down. I love Target,
like LOVE me some Target. It is my retail therapy drug of choice.
Most of the time, when I head in there I grab a cart because let's be
real—I don't tell Target what I need. It tells me. For whatever reason, I recently entered the mechanical doors and grabbed nothing.
No basket. No cart. I just waltzed in empty-handed. I needed two
things: Mucinex for the kiddo and vitamins. I'd be in and out. We
all know where this is headed, right?

I grabbed the items I needed but then remembered I could use
some more K-cups. So, I made my way back to the food section,
which of course, led me right past the makeup aisles, which reminded me I needed hairspray. When I looked to my right, I saw

the cute desk organizer crap I didn't need, so I decided maybe I needed some new office supplies. Oh, look, a new runner! That's cute. By the time I made it to the back of the store, I was threading things through my fingers, stacking items up to my chin, and praying I didn't drop anything, including the bath mat I didn't need.

It was real-life Tetris, and I was losing. Things were falling, and people kept stopping to ask if I needed help. "Do you need a cart, or can I get you a basket?"

"Nope, I got it," I replied, scooping up the fallen items while sweating through my coat.

I was committed to carrying it all. No matter how completely unmanageable it was, I refused anyone's help. Target plays the game well; they even have basket racks scattered throughout the store in anticipation that we may bite off more than we can chew. I passed every one of them with a scowl. The thought of lightening my load was not an option. If I attempted to set something down the whole thing would crumble, so I fumbled my way through the store to the checkout.

Our burdens are like the items I was carrying. Whether we care to admit it or not, we all have them. Burdens are constant and inevitable. Maybe not for you at this moment, but perhaps they were in the past or will be in the future. Sometimes it's from circumstances out of our control, while other times, it is self-imposed. We over-commit and set unrealistic expectations. We forget the cart, scoff at the basket, and outright refuse the help. We fill our arms until we physically can't carry anything else.

Isn't that the same for so many of us? It's important to understand that burdens come in all shapes and sizes. Sometimes they're emotional, while other times, they're physical or mental, financial or health-related, or external factors. Even our past traumas, those things that are deeply rooted within our own personal experiences and things we are going through, can spin up when we least expect it, but we don't need to carry them on our own. It's okay to call a friend and say, "Do you have five minutes for me to vent? Are you in a good place right now where you can hear this?"

We have to push past this idea that we must internalize it all. Having burdens doesn't make you a burden. Read that again, because you need it to sink in: Having burdens doesn't make you a burden.

I know what it's like to feel as though we're doing ourselves a favor by isolating ourselves and keeping it in, but it actually has the opposite effect. When we don't allow ourselves to release the burden, our emotions mount up and the load becomes heavier. I get it; it's scary to be vulnerable, to be fearful of judgment while shouldering a heavy load, but it's okay to share our burdens. After all, our struggles are what connect us; they deepen friendships and strengthen bonds. If a friend called you with an issue, I guarantee none of us would think, Wow, what a burden! I can't believe you wasted my time. We'd be grateful that they entrusted us with it, yet we fail to give ourselves the same grace to let go. Even if we're not reducing the burdens, carrying them together makes it easier. We can offer a listening ear, or a shoulder to lean on. We can bring over a meal, or help a friend by taking their kid to practice.

By openly denying someone an opportunity to be there, it's not fair to yourself or the person offering to help. My husband can read me like a book. It drives me absolutely insane, but it also has saved me from myself many times. When I'm stressed, he asks, "How can I help? What can I take off your plate right now to lighten your load?" I used to say there was nothing he could do, but now I realize it's okay to lay some things in his arms. I don't have to carry it all myself. Now I respond by handing him a list of items I need from the grocery store, or he grabs the kiddo without me asking and tells me to get whatever I need to do done. There are always areas where we can look for help. If you're shuffling kids halfway across town to swimming and dance, it shouldn't be your responsibility to also figure out what everyone's eating for the night. Tell people what you need. Call your mom, phone a friend, or tell your husband.

The relief we feel when releasing a burden is profound. I distinctly remember the text exchange I had with one of my best friends about my son's surgery and the weight that was consuming me. A trip home after surgery was next to impossible, so we opted to stay in a hotel in case any issues arose.

"I'm scared. I don't know that Jim and I can do this alone. We're two and a half hours away from home. What if something goes wrong?" I typed, wiping tears from my face.

"I truly don't know how you are carrying it all right now," she responded. "As your friend, but also a mother, I can't imagine the fear you're experiencing. Just know that I'm here. We're praying for you all every single day. I've got some goodies coming in the mail for G, and one for you, too. Love you."

I could feel the weight in my chest release. For a moment, the tenseness in my shoulders melted away. She offered me space, and in doing so, she was shouldering the burden with me. She was lightening my load. While she may not have been physically there for me, she could be, emotionally.

The gift she gave me was a coffee mug with a quote on it about strength. A gentle reminder that while we can do hard things, we're not meant to do them alone. Sis checked in on me countless times over the course of those few weeks, as did many of my other friends. My mom brought over some meals and treats to help lighten the load too, because that's what we do. We all carry burdens, but the beautiful thing is we don't have to carry them alone.

When you find yourself in hard times and you can't feel your way out of it, and it seems as though there are not enough tears available to cry, ask yourself: What am I struggling with today? And more importantly, how can someone help? You don't have to go through life thinking it's better if you just carry it all. You only have two hands. You can grab a cart. You can phone a friend or text your family. You can schedule a therapy session to help you process your feelings.

You don't have to carry it all. It's okay to sometimes let others carry you.

MOVING FORWARD

We all hold on to too much, both personally and professionally. What is something you've been carrying with you that may be weighing you down? (i.e.: a grudge, diagnosis, obligation, or regret)

How can you work to lighten your load? What can you let go of? Identify three things you've been carrying, that you could give to someone else. Notice how it makes you feel when you give yourself permission to put those things down and ask for help.

Do you know someone who is struggling with burdens? In what way are you able to reach out to help them?

Chapter 10

Greater Expectations

Failure Belief: I can't lower the bar

At thirty years old, my jaw nearly locked shut. For someone who loves to talk and relies on it to do my job, this was a big problem. I was on week one of a three-week travel stint for work. We were gearing up for one of the largest tradeshows of the year, and I had hundreds of people to talk to. It was an event where companies and businesses gathered to showcase their products and services to potential clients and customers. As I stared in the mirror of my Vegas hotel bathroom, I popped a few ibuprofen to numb the pain and prayed that the swelling in my face would go down. I looked like a chipmunk with my cheeks all puffy.

I washed my face, my eyes still swollen from the 12-hour long work day before. As I plugged in my curling iron and began brushing my hair, a large clump hit the ground. To be clear, my hair grows like a freaking Chia Pet and I shed like an Alaskan Malamute, so a clump or two of hair here and there is fairly normal. But as I kept brushing, the hair kept falling out.

WTH? Isn't this crap only supposed to happen when I'm fifty? Am I sick? What is wrong with me?

As panic set in, I quickly applied my makeup and called my mom while curling my hair.

"Mom, I can barely move my jaw," I said, fighting back tears. "I don't know what to do. It hurts to even talk."

"Have you taken any ibuprofen?" she asked.

"Yeah, I just did," I replied.

"Good," she said. "Take it around the clock and ice your jaw whenever you can to help with the inflammation. Call the dentist and make an appointment for when you come back. And don't just blow me off. I'm serious. You're under a lot of stress, and if you don't get it under control it may lock completely. Take some deep breaths."

As I meandered my way to the edge of the bed, trying my best to take my mom's advice and destress, I glanced at the clock. 6:05 a.m. Time to get dressed and head down to the lobby. The call to the doctor would have to wait. I needed to grab a coffee and a cab.

For the next week, my jaw continued to bump and grind more than a 90's R&B song.

After Vegas, I flew to Arizona for a week and a half to finish our customer program. There's something about the desert, Native American flute music playing throughout the resort, and good guacamole that calms the soul. It was just what I needed after two fast-paced weeks in Vegas.

When I got home, my doctor referred me to a specialist. It turns out the culprit really was stress. Countless x-rays and a giant bill later, I was informed that arthritis had taken residency in my jaw from grinding and clenching my teeth, all because of stress, which meant a lifetime of pain and only one way to mediate it—headgear.

You read that right. And no, I'm not talking about a simple Invisalign retainer. Believe me, I wish I was. Think bulkier and speech-limiting. My doctor affectionately calls it my appliance. Remember that scene from Sixteen Candles where the geek is asleep in the back of Jake's convertible parked in Caroline's church parking lot? Please for the love, tell me you've seen this movie. I'm a 90's kid, okay? Just go with it. Anyways, Caroline slaps his cheek to wake him and he mumbles, "Dang, Mom, I got my headgear on." That's me. Laugh all you want, but it's where I'm at right now.

All jokes aside, at just thirty, I was carrying so much stress that my body was screaming out in pain. This was supposed to be my dream job. I was planning events and jet-setting across the country, all while answering emails at 2:00 a.m. By society's standards, I had made it. However, I quickly realized that 14-hour days and sleep deprivation only get you hair loss and arthritis. But I was willing to do it all anyway.

It was buck up or shut up. If I couldn't do the job now, what made me think I could handle it while being a working mom?

Eight years later, I'm still rocking the headgear. My husband likes to poke fun and remind me of how ridiculous I sound. He says my retainer is, "Schuper cool."

But every time I try to go a day or so without it, I feel like my jaw is being ripped apart when I open my mouth to talk. Why? Because the stress never went away. Sure, it changed and manifested into other things and different areas of my life, but it's still there. Half of the time I don't even realize I'm stressed.

As women and mothers, our bodies are in a constant state of fight or flight. We work in defense mode, always on our A-game. We deflect, protect, internalize, and run ourselves ragged. We ignore all signs our bodies give us, telling us to slow down or change course. We simply keep pushing, hanging on by a thread.

But if I'm being truthful, the headgear is a Band-Aid. A temporary fix to a much larger problem. Society tells us that women need to do it all, and if you're having a hard time getting there, then quite frankly, it's you. Be a little more selfless. You're clearly not giving enough of yourself. It's all or nothing, ladies. We need perfection.

So, we try to give the world what it wants, and we wear ourselves out in the process. We cram in a one-hour yoga session a week as if somehow that will remove years of stress. Our cortisol levels are through the roof, and our jeans keep getting tighter, and we can't figure out why.

The problem: Society is full of crap. Stress is never going to go away, especially when you are willing to sacrifice every ounce of yourself in the process just because some random person on the internet told you you should.

It's okay if you can't do it all. It's okay to stand up and say, I don't need your made-up ideals. I'm good where I'm at. You don't have to answer the email at 2:00 a.m. to be a good employee. You don't have to register your kids for every traveling team under the sun in order to be a good mom. You don't have to sign up for every church meal train that hits your inbox and be active at the local MOPS (Mothers of Preschoolers) group to be a good person. You don't have to do any of it.

I know right now you're thinking, woman, have you lost your mind? Do you know what people will say if I don't do all those things? But I'm telling you, it doesn't matter. None of it. What matters is that you recognize that you control your bar. You control the level of expectations and stress in your life. Not your mother-in-law or your boss. Not your co-worker or your friends. YOU.

I get it, I really do. I'm a perfectionist by nature. But, if motherhood has taught me anything, it's the reality that I will never be able to do it all. Perfection is a myth. It's not attainable. It's debilitating. It strips us of our joy and leaves us feeling tense. I tried for years to be the poster child of perfection and look where it's gotten me. I'll be wearing headgear until it's replaced by dentures. I took on more and more and pushed myself to the limit until I did so much irreversible damage to my jaw that it will never be the same. I'm not proud of it.

But I understand now that whatever level of expectation I have of myself, it's my own. I control the bar, and so do you. Lower it. Take the whole dang thing off if you want to. Have a burn party in your backyard and roast the sucker for all I care. Yes, it's okay if the towels need to be folded a certain way, and you'd rather just do it yourself than watch them be folded incorrectly. But what's not okay is when those things and those expectations you carry start to weigh you down and cost you your sanity.

Today we make a truce to ourselves. A truce to protect our own energy and time. Today we start by choosing to set the bar at a more realistic height. A height determined by our own standards, headgear and all.

~~~~~~

MOVING FORWARD

What expectations do I have of myself? Are they realistic?

Our expectations can create pressure and hinder our own happiness without even realizing it. What areas of your life do you feel the most stress? (i.e., work, kids, marriage, family, cleaning, etc.)

In what ways can you lower the bar to something more attainable and manageable in those areas to combat stress?

Are your expectations strictly yours, or have they been inherited by society?

~~~~~~

Chapter 11

Mommysaurus Rex

Failure Belief: Good moms never yell

I yelled today. I could blame it on the glass of milk my son spilled all over the table this morning for the fourth time this week or the mess that seems to accumulate the second anyone is awake, but I'd be lying. It wasn't the milk or the mess I had to clean up. It wasn't the piles of laundry I failed to get to for the second day in a row or the dishes strung across the counter from the night before. It wasn't the consistent lack of sleep for four years straight or the pinched nerve in my back that continually reminded me I need to prioritize myself better. Nor was it the fact that despite my best efforts, I never managed to get caught up no matter how much I did or how thin I spread myself.

It was a culmination of things. Like those icebergs you see in photographs, where only a small portion protrudes above the water while a giant mass lurks beneath the surface, the same could be said for my stress level. My patience was hanging on by a thread. Today the milk happened to be the thing that derailed us just enough to throw our trajectory off course and puncture the boat.

"Don't spill," I said, placing the red cup on the table. "I filled it high, so be careful."

"Okay, Mommy," my son replied, setting his dinosaur down next to him, his feet swinging back and forth beneath the table.

I made my way to the sink and began rinsing the dishes I failed to load in the dishwasher the night before. I glanced over at my four-year-old, who sat blissfully in the chair, playing with his dinosaur instead of eating, like I had asked.

"Bug, what did Mommy say about toys at the table? Put the dinosaur down. I need you to eat." I went back to loading the dishwasher, and that's when I heard it. The clang of a plastic cup hitting the table.

Like a slow-motion scene in your favorite 90's movie, I turned around to see a river of white milk everywhere.

"Uh-oh," my son said with his dinosaur in hand. "It was an accident."

"You've GOT to be kidding me!!!" I said, frantically pulling off paper towels. "This is the fourth time you've done this. You should be able to drink out of a regular cup by now. Why can't you be more careful?"

His sweet face stared back at me blankly as I tested the limit of the Bounty's absorbency. My lack of patience at that moment was utterly ridiculous, and I knew it. But I couldn't stop my frustrations from bursting out.

I always thought I would be a cool mom. Even keeled, never hot out of the gate, always patient and fun-loving. I had it all mapped out. I knew exactly who I was and the mom I was going to be. Except that always patient part? It turns out I wasn't really great at nailing it. I suppress too much, and my patience suffers because of it.

I'm well aware that there are people who have the patience of a saint. As nauseating as that is, I know it exists because I've seen it. Their version of yelling is raising their voice one decibel while still somehow remaining calm and tossing up flower petals. I, unfortunately, am not one of those people. If my voice doesn't tell you how much you're in trouble, my facial expressions will. There is a reason my husband calls me mommysaurus rex.

I bury things way down deep and press on. I ignore and pretend everything is fine when inside a battle is raging. But rather than acknowledging my feelings, I take on more tasks. I pile it on and pile it on, thinking somehow it will make me feel better and more accomplished. I spread myself thinner and thinner until some unexpected thing inserting itself into my day sends me spiraling into tears and words of frustration. All patience ceases to exist.

And then, I rage clean. Yeah, that's a thing. At least for me, anyway. I scrub counters until they are shiny enough to see my reflection. For whatever reason, it gives me some weird sense of control in a world seemingly spinning into chaos.

While huffing, puffing, and tearing through half a roll of paper towels, I apologized to my little guy. "I'm sorry, bug. I didn't mean to yell. Mommy is just frustrated and tired. I shouldn't have taken it out on you."

"It's okay, Mommy. I'm sorry I made a mess," he said with his sad baby blue eyes filled with tears. "Are you mad?"

How could I be mad at my four-year-old? Accidents happen, and things get spilled. If anyone needed to be asking the question, are you mad? it should've been me. Instead, I let my emotions get the best of me, per usual, and instantly felt nothing but guilt. This wasn't the mom I had envisioned I would be, and no matter how many times I tell myself that today is going to be different, something inevitably gets screwed up, and I fall short yet again.

We all know the spilled milk was never the problem. Heck, I think even my four-year-old could tell at that point that it had nothing to do with him. We bottle it up and choke our emotions down until we can barely breathe. Then it spews all over the ones we love.

But I'm slowly learning that when we recognize the response for what it really is, we begin to acknowledge our emotions. We allow ourselves room to process the very things we so often suppress. When we lose it on our kids and get angry, it's because something triggered us emotionally. Instead of processing those feelings of anger, we transform them into a reaction of emotional outbursts. Take the spilled milk, for example. Could I have benefited from walking away from the situation and giving myself a few minutes?

Absolutely, but not without a river of milk cascading onto my hardwood floors. So, I reacted angrily. Don't get me wrong—I was completely annoyed at having to clean up milk yet again, but the milk was simply the emotional trigger. The trigger for the fact I was already overwhelmed, due to my lack of control and inability to grapple with or make sense of anything in my life. It was about me and what I couldn't get a handle on.

Talk about a gut check. Hello, emotional intelligence. It's nice to meet you. Yes, I am, a grown adult who still fails to allow myself space to identify my emotions and manage them accordingly. Can you relate?

In a recent article I read in The Washington Post, clinical psychologist and author of The Tantrum Survival Guide, Rebecca Schrag Hershberg, says, "In my clinical and personal experience, yelling goes hand in hand with overwhelm. Something about the situation is overwhelming for parents, whether it's a time crunch or a long and exhausting day separate from parenting. We don't yell when we feel calm and regulated."

Can you identify with this? Maybe today you're having one of those days. Maybe this morning the wheels came off and the kids were screaming while the oldest decided to give the baby a haircut when you weren't looking. There are Cheerios on the floor, and you just realized you're out of diapers. Rather than allow yourself space to process and breathe through your anger and frustrations, you react. You lose it. You yell and bang cabinet doors. You demand shoes be found, and issue threats like no one's business. You officially declare mommy law, then have instant regret.

I threw the milk-soaked paper towels into the garbage and walked over to my son, who was standing in the living room. I knelt down and placed his hands into mine.

"Baby, look at me. Mommy isn't mad at you. I know it was an accident," I said, pulling him in for a hug. "I'm sorry. I know I'm not the best mommy in the world, but I will always apologize when I mess up. I love you."

He smiled as he lifted his head from my shoulder. "I love you too, Mommy. It's okay. I forgive you. I'm going to make you a surprise!"

I went into the office to answer a few emails before heading out the door for school drop-off. After a few minutes, he came in. His tiny hands holding a pink post-it note that read:

I love you and evre time you git mad I frgiv you mommy.

Love Grady

It sits at my desk to this day as a reminder that we all make mistakes. It's not just you. It happens to all of us. It doesn't mean you've failed. It doesn't classify you as the world's worst mom, even though I know it feels like it in the moment. It makes you human. The guilt you feel after yelling is your emotional intelligence kicking in. It's as if your brain is throwing a red flag, saying, "Whoa. You feel this way because of how you reacted. Breathe and apologize." Having emotional intelligence doesn't mean you're suddenly going to descend into a euphoric state of constant peace. It's knowing and equipping yourself with the tools necessary to practice responding with intention. You won't wake up and never yell again; that's simply not realistic. What you can do is be more aware, and intentional, with how and when you do respond to situations that may trigger you.

By acknowledging our mistakes, we teach our children how to process emotions and work through our feelings through love and forgiveness. We show them the importance of apologizing, and what it means to be accountable for our actions. They see our imperfections on full display, but also the value and courage it takes to own them, and the growth that happens when we do. In us, they are reminded that we can be loved as we are. Our humanness is not our downfall, but our saving grace. The one true thing that connects us and reminds us we were never meant to be perfect; we're human.

We're all a work in progress. Some of us just go through a few more paper towels to clean up the mess. Which reminds me, I better add some more to the grocery list.

~~~~~~

MOVING FORWARD

Stress presents itself in various forms, often creating knee-jerk reactions and responses. What stressors and/or triggers send you reeling? (i.e.: running late, kids fighting, power struggles, being ignored, exhaustion, feelings of judgment and/or embarrassment, etc.)

Now that you've identified a few emotional triggers, what are some tangible ways you can help yourself in those moments?

The next time you find yourself wanting to yell, pause, and allow yourself time to examine why you feel this way. Are you trying to do too much? Is your anger a reasonable response, or is there an unresolved issue that needs to be acknowledged?

~~~~~~

Chapter 12

The Answer Is No

Failure Belief: I need to say "yes" to everything

I used to be a "yes" girl. A rule follower to a fault. A square. My husband would argue I'm still as naïve as they come, but I'm getting better at pushing the limits. For the longest time, pleasing those around me was my job, and I was good at it. Never one to disappoint, I knew exactly what everyone wanted from me and how I was supposed to go about it. Perfection was my jam. After all, girls are supposed to mind their P's and Q's. We're taught from an early age to be quiet and pleasant, to dial down our voices in a concerted effort to please others and be deemed worthy. Phrases like: "Don't make waves." "Try not to be so difficult." "Just go along with it" are hardcoded into our internal psyche and we don't even know it. We learn all too quickly how to be innately in tune with the needs of those around us, and how to say "yes" to everything, even at the expense of our own passions and desires.

I know because I was one of them. I was good at making people happy. I was good at seeing a need and always extending a hand and a yes. And for the longest time, it made me feel good. It validated my existence and made me feel worthy—until one day, it didn't. Until the very idea of saying yes to one more thing left me feeling emotionally depleted, on edge, and lost. Up until now, I had tied my self-worth to being everything to everyone. My sole purpose of existence was to serve and seek the love of others. I wanted and needed to do it all, but there was one caveat: My all was never enough.

I was drowning in motherhood, life, and work. I was tackling it all, saying "yes" to all the things, when on the inside, my body was screaming for me to stop. I knew I couldn't keep going at this pace, but I didn't want to let anyone down. The irony of it all was that by saying yes to everything, I wasn't helping anyone. I was stretched too thin, running at a snail's pace, fueled by coffee and a miracle. I needed a break, so I scheduled a massage at our local high-end spa. Something about stepping into that place made me feel instantly at ease. Maybe it was the flute music, hot tea, and energy trail mix, or the chance to read in silence while the oversized robe seemed to swallow my body whole, but whatever it was, I had been looking forward to this moment all day.

"Hi, Jennifer. My name is Candace. I'll be doing your Swedish massage today. Come on back and we'll get you started."

As we entered the room, she prompted me where to put my things and asked which oil scent I preferred. "I'll step outside so you can get ready, and I'll be back in a moment to check on you."

When the door shut, I scrambled quickly to hang my robe and hop onto the table, making an effort to not jack up the perfectly folded sheet coverings. As I sunk into the table, I breathed a sigh of relief. Candace entered the room, quietly placing an eye mask over my eyes while guiding me through a few deep breaths. Those first few minutes were bliss, but then...

My Swedish massage felt more like a deep-tissue torture of death. Every touch felt like the pressure was going to send me screaming. My face winced in pain as the massage went on.

"Is the pressure, okay?" she asked.

"Yes," I replied.

Yes?! I can think of a lot of words to use, and yes is definitely not the one that comes to mind. Really, Jenn. Just say something. No. What if I offend her? I mean other people must enjoy this kind of pressure. Just take it. Don't be rude.

So, I did. I paid $98 plus tip for a massage I hated, all because I didn't want to offend someone. Something that was meant to relax me left me feeling miserable and sore. I created my own personal massage hell because I didn't want to speak up. I was afraid of conflict and feared hurting a stranger's feelings.

A few weeks later, I received an email regarding a business opportunity that under normal circumstances, I would have loved to pursue, but the timing wasn't right. I knew it, but it didn't matter. Every ounce of me still wanted to say yes. Why? Because I was more concerned about how it would be perceived if I declined.

An email that was literally a mere three sentences long took me close to two hours to draft and another forty seconds to actually hit send. During that entire time, I wanted to cry. I erased and rephrased. I overanalyzed and critiqued word placement and tone. I read and re-read, paused, hovered over send, and then re-read again.

My husband looked at me while I fretted on the couch, my fingers nervously drumming over the keyboard of my laptop. "What's the problem?" he asked.

Ah, a chance for feedback! "I don't know, does this sound okay? It feels kind of abrupt to me. Like, too matter of fact. Can I read it to you again?"

"No. We've been over this. What you have is fine. Just hit send and be done with it."

I'm sorry, come again? You want me to just hit send and be done with it?!?! I'm not sure you remember who you are married to, but that is not how we do things here. You know this. I mean, yes, in some alternate universe, my husband was right, but I never mutter those words out loud. Are you kidding me? I think I've said them maybe twice in our marriage; one of which he actually recorded for later reference and, I can only assume, blackmail.

Clearly, he was right, and I had, after all, read it to him five times. His no was unacceptable, though. It needed to be a polite no. You know those boxes you see on TV or in Facebook ads where the mom opens the package and surprise butterflies come out? Yeah, more like that. I want a no with sunshine and rainbows. Maybe even a few pops of confetti. I want a no that says no but feels like a yes. It would sit better and make me feel less like garbage.

And since he wasn't supplying me with the reassurance and answer I needed, I did what any girl in my shoes would do: I phoned a friend, and not just any friend, but one who would analyze it with me but still shoot straight. I explained the situation and the details around the opportunity itself. Her response was, "Given everything you have on your plate right now, is this truly worth your time and energy?"

"No, but how do I politely decline? I feel like I wasted their time," I said. "I sat on a call with them to inquire more about the opportunity, said I was interested, and now I'm declining. I feel like an idiot."

Then she took me to school as only she can. "This is exactly where we as women need to reframe our thinking. Nothing you did was out of line or a waste of time. You inquired about the opportunity, thought you might be interested, and decided the timing just isn't right. Saying no isn't a bad thing; it's establishing healthy boundaries and protecting your energy."

WHOA. You want me to protect my energy? Women don't say no. We apologize relentlessly and say yes to all the things, regardless if our plate is full.

She was right. Up until a few years ago, I said yes to everything. You need me at 2:00 a.m., I'm your girl. Need that report in 30 minutes, I'll get right on that. Oh, that date doesn't work for you? I'll reschedule for something more convenient for you.

As I sat on the phone, I thought for a bit. "So, what should I write?" I asked.

"It doesn't need to be anything elaborate," she explained. "Just something like, thank you for sending this over. I really appreciate the opportunity to talk with you this morning. After looking at the attached proposal, I don't think this is a project I can commit to at this time. Maybe we will find a time in the future that works for both of us. Thank you again."

"That's it? I don't need to explain why I'm declining?"

"Nothing you say is going to change the outcome," she said. "The answer is still no, regardless. You don't owe anyone an explanation. If they want to know more, they will ask for more details."

And with that, I hit send. It was hard, and I hated every minute of it, but I knew it was the right thing to do. And you know what? No one died. The earth didn't stop turning, and no one's feelings were shattered that day. I even got a response back thanking me for my honesty.

No. Such a simple word, riddled with anxiety and fear.

From the moment we are born, we're taught to say our pleases and thank yous. We're reminded to be polite and always share. Societal standards have labeled women the peacemakers, and we fulfill that role, oftentimes willingly, while others do it begrudgingly. We push aside our own needs to ensure those around us are happy every single day. But at what cost?

I share these two stories to show you both extremes. Our inability to say no is woven into everything we do, from small everyday things like massages or the color of our pedicures to large life-altering decisions like careers. As women, we've been socialized into silence. The idea of someone being angry or critical of us creates fear and tension. So much so, that I was willing to forgo my own health and sanity because it pleased someone else, even if that person was someone I didn't even know. It didn't matter that it was the wrong choice for me and every ounce of my body was telling me not to do it. I was ready to say yes.

Have you been there? How many times in a day do you catch yourself saying "yes" to things you don't even want to?

Our desire to please those around us in an effort to seek love is one that begins in early adolescence and continues into adulthood. We believe the word no to be a dirty word that requires us to explain or rationalize our reasoning, so we avoid it at all costs. Instead, we reach for conformity in an effort to create restitute over conflict. But psychologist and author, Dr. Shefali, says, "By saying no, we are acknowledging this doesn't feel right to me, and I need to stop participating in it. We do this by saying no through our words or our actions. The no isn't to the other person, per se. It's to ourselves. We say no to the roles we have robotically and unconsciously played in the past. It's not about asking the other person to change. It just demands that we stop our participation in the dynamic."

Oof, talk about a gut punch. She's right. Instead of respecting ourselves and saying no, we ignore our inner peace to meet the expectations of those around us. We sign up for the thing or say "yes" to yet another family function, even when every bone in our body is telling us not to. We agree to sushi with a friend, despite our disdain for raw fish and borderline shellfish allergy. We say "yes" to another date with a guy we're not even into because we don't want to be mean. Your friends said he's super nice, so what would that make you? We plan the extravagant wedding to meet our families' expectations when truthfully, we just want something small. We sit silently in the conference room, disagreeing with everything being said, yet fail to speak up for fear of ruffling feathers.

When I truly stepped back and examined all the times I silenced my own inner knowing and chose to say yes, instead of honoring myself, I felt sick to my stomach. Why do we do this to ourselves? Why do we continually say yes to things that don't even serve us? I'll tell you—because we know no other way. It's been ingrained in women since birth that prioritizing our own desires is somehow selfish. Our likeability depends on our willingness to bend. Think about it. How many times have you come across a woman who was outspoken and unafraid to say no? What was your initial reaction? While some of us may find a woman's confidence empowering, most of us tend to think she must be bossy or a bitch, right? Women don't speak up like that. Who does she think she is? She must be completely full of herself. And yet, when men speak with assertiveness, they are met with praise. He's a leader. A natural-born CEO.

Do you hear your own biases? Do you sense the years of ingrained gender stereotypes? We live in the twenty-first century, and yet so many of us still struggle with people-pleasing. We willingly accept the role of martyr by editing ourselves for the consumption of others. We give and avoid. We renounce and reject confrontation. We seek to appease at all costs. Quite simply, we set ourselves on fire to keep others warm, and we don't even question why before lighting the match. We operate on this limitless mentality, but it's not without consequences.

The limit does exist. The limit is you. You don't always have to keep the peace. If something makes you uncomfortable, you can say no. If you don't believe an idea at work is going in the right direction, it's okay to disagree. You don't always have to check the sign-up box for the PTA or the latest school activity. You can sit some things out. You can do things that fill your cup.

The good news is that by authentically knowing ourselves we can unlearn our habits. Trust me when I tell you, not everyone is going to like this "new" you: one that no longer is intertwined and leaning on others to provide you with a sense of worth. Instead, you're more in tune with what serves you and what doesn't, because you recognize your limits and what you need. The reality is when you do this, others may not agree with your choices, but that is a reflection of them, not you. If someone is angry with you for saying no, it's most likely because it requires more of them, or their projected expectations aren't being met. They're unsure of how to react to this new you because they've become accustomed to you meeting and fulfilling their needs.

But saying "yes" should never be our default answer. Of course, it's good to respect others and not seek to harm anyone, but when a yes requires self-sacrifice and annihilation of our own values and mental well-being, we must change course.

The voice in the back of your mind saying this date should probably end right now...listen to it. Your subconscious is telling you to not take the risk. Speak up. If you don't like the way they cooked your steak, don't say "yes, everything is great," knowing you feel like the dang thing is still mooing. Say "no" and send it back. Stop accepting that the only answer is yes.

I know it's hard to retrain your brain to think counter to what you've been taught your whole life, believe me. I was a "yes" girl. But now, with every no, I inch closer to protecting my own energy and time, and you will too. Start small. Practice saying no to every-day things. The refill on your cup of coffee, or the dessert you don't want. The guy in the automotive department trying to charge you for ten more things when all you want is an oil change. Your friend who wants to meet for drinks at the bar, but it's 10:00 p.m., and you're in your PJs.

Be firm and confident in your response, and remember that you don't always need to give an explanation. Sometimes the answer is simply no. The first few times you utter these words, it will make you uncomfortable, but as you continue, it will become easier and less anxiety-ridden. You begin to understand that saying no doesn't make you a bad person. It makes you strong and more aware. It means you place your energy and your wellbeing within the same spectrum you do everyone else. You are now driven by your inner knowing as opposed to the needs and expectations others project on you.

Listen to your inner voice. Pay attention to what you say yes to and, especially, why. Are you saying yes out of fear and rejection, or yes because it feels good? A yes needs to be a full-body yes, and a no does too. How do you feel? Is your inner self screaming for you to stop? Make sure your response aligns with who you are. You don't have to always keep the peace and be everything for everyone, but you do need to keep the peace within yourself. Sometimes that requires us to say one simple word. No.

MOVING FORWARD

Take a few minutes to identify your priorities. What does your inner self truly value?

How can you better protect your peace? What things are taking space that you need to be better at saying "no" to?

What have you said "yes" to recently or in the past that didn't align with your values? How did that make you feel? How could you have responded differently?

What are some responses we can practice to stand firm when we know it doesn't serve us? (i.e.: I appreciate the offer, but I'm at capacity. I won't be able to make it.)

HOW WE SEE OUR BODIES

Chapter 13

Ruffling Feathers

Failure Belief: I don't know how to set good boundaries

I remember the first time I had flowers delivered to work. All of the ladies quickly clamored around my desk, attempting to catch a sneak peek at who they were from.

"Are they from your boyfriend?" one asked.

"What's the special occasion?" inquired another. "I've been trying to get my husband to send me flowers for years. He still hasn't gotten the hint."

I fumbled with the envelope as I attempted to read the card inside. It was a thank you note for booking a conference room from one of my colleagues. A male colleague. I wanted to die. I could feel my face reddening with both rage and utter embarrassment. Now what am I supposed to say?

"So, who's it from?" they insisted.

"Oh, just some flowers from a friend. Don't you all have a meeting you're supposed to be in?" I nervously managed to smile, trying desperately to change the subject.

Thankfully, it worked. As soon as they left, I ripped the card to shreds and threw it in the trash. I wanted to toss the flowers right along with it or burn them, I wasn't sure which. Either way, I wanted to cry or maybe throw up. Do I go to HR? I mean, this is so inappropriate. Who sends flowers to someone for booking a conference room? It's literally part of my job. No. You are not going to be THAT, girl. Suck it up.

I opened up my messenger app for work.

"Hey. Why did you send me flowers for doing my job?" I asked.

"I just wanted to say thank you. You helped me out in a pinch and I greatly appreciated it, that's all. I hope you like them," he replied.

"Well, it wasn't necessary. You said thank you. That's good enough."

"Relax, I didn't mean anything by it," he typed back.

You're overreacting, Jenn. I mean, he has a wife and kids at home. Clearly, he wasn't trying to be inappropriate. He even said so. Maybe he's just uber-friendly and expressive. Just let it go.

So I did, or at least I tried, but I couldn't shake the nagging feeling that it was completely wrong and inappropriate. I took the flowers that night and chucked them in the trash as I walked to the parking garage. I didn't want to look at them.

Over the next few weeks, everything at work was normal. I was relieved. I remained cordial and attempted to maintain my business-as-usual mentality. And then a message appeared on my screen from the same guy.

"Your smile is the highlight of my day. I don't think you know how beautiful you are."

I sat there staring at my monitor in disbelief. I felt sick to my stomach. How could this be happening? What do I do?

"Please stop," I typed back as my hands shook. I immediately put myself on "do not disturb mode" and tried to pretend it wasn't happening.

The next morning he walked past my desk and placed two bottles of Victoria's Secret lotion on the counter.

"I saw these, and the smell reminded me of you. I thought you would like them."

I could feel every part of my body pop out in a sweat.

"I don't use lotion," I said.

"Keep it for the team then. Someone may want to use it," he said with a smile.

My boss was watching the whole encounter from his office window. He walked up immediately after with a peculiar look on his face.

"What's this all about?" he said, picking up one of the bottles.

"I have no idea. I've asked him to stop. He keeps messaging me and giving me things. The flowers from a few weeks ago were from him, too. I don't know what to do."

"Handle it," my boss said as he turned and went back to his office.

That was it. Two words. Not, "I'll have a talk with him," or "maybe you should go to HR," just, "handle it." As if somehow all of this was my fault.

I opened messenger again. The thought of going to his desk and having to discuss this face-to-face made my skin want to crawl.

"Please stop. You are making me uncomfortable," I typed. I hit send and blocked his name. I didn't want to see his response. I didn't care what the excuse was because there wasn't an acceptable one. What he was doing was completely inappropriate.

A few days passed with no instances. I prayed he had gotten the message. As he walked past my desk on one particular morning, he stopped.

"I feel like you're ignoring me," he said.

I leaned forward, hands shaking. "You know why. I am not okay with what you are doing. Just please stop. I'm not going to ask you again," I said, quietly attempting to keep anyone within earshot from hearing.

"Okay then," he replied, looking at me as if I were crazy.

At the time, I thought maybe I was crazy. He sure made me feel like it. As if I somehow imagined it all. Maybe I was making it into a bigger deal than it really was. I don't know. All I knew was that I needed it to stop. The emotional toll and stress it was causing was debilitating. I dreaded coming to work each day for fear of what I may encounter.

Thankfully, after that, it stopped. Looking back, I now see how bad the situation really was, yet I never truly used my voice. Sure, I asked the question as to why the flowers were sent, and I eventually told him to stop, but I allowed him to manipulate me into thinking I was overreacting. I knew. My instincts were telling me that this wasn't okay, but I ignored them out of fear of being "that" woman. I didn't want to ruffle feathers or get someone in trouble. I was too concerned about being polite and nice, even when my own personal boundaries were being compromised. I worried that I had done something to provoke his advances or that I was somehow in the wrong. I didn't want to be seen as accusatory.

We all have personal limits. Thresholds we know and wish to uphold, yet we consistently let others cross them. Sometimes it's physical. Other times it's emotional, mental, or time-related boundaries. Maybe it's a family member who doesn't align and agree with your life choices, or an inappropriate co-worker who says offensive things. Maybe it's a friend who takes advantage of you and continually asks for favors or money. Maybe your workplace doesn't respect your time and constantly expects you to work long hours. Maybe your mother-in-law routinely stops in unannounced or interjects her opinions about your parenting style.

Whatever it is, what stops us from speaking up? I'll tell you. Our society has routinely labeled women as peacemakers. We're expected to be nurturing and dependent. Soft-spoken and weak. There are no lines drawn in the sand around our boundaries because we have none. Women, by design, exist to fit and fulfill the needs of others; or so we're taught. We naively think and hope that others will see us as equal, or better yet, simply respect our existence and autonomy.

But boundaries are needed not just for ourselves, but for teaching others how we want and expect to be treated. The very definition of the word boundaries means a line that marks the limit in which something should not cross. It's the space we wish to protect. The circle we create around ourselves to safeguard our time, energy, values, dignity, mental well-being, and bodies. You get to decide and set the placeholders for those boundaries. We get to choose what crosses the line and what doesn't, but it's up to us to enforce them. When we don't, we give others the green light to dictate and cross those boundaries for us.

In an article written for the Harvard Business Review by Joe Sanok, he says, "Boundaries are all about who we give power to. They force us to analyze why we may not be giving ourselves permission to work and live in the way that we feel is best for our well-being. If we're not deciding our lives, schedules, and workloads, who is? Boundaries allow us to decide when, how, and if we give this power away."

Those few sentences shook me to my core. So how do we get better at implementing them? The first step is to acknowledge that often times boundaries are crossed most frequently by those closest to us. Perhaps it's a family member, a close friend, or sometimes our own partners. Beyond that, boundaries can be intersected by bosses, colleagues, acquaintances, and even strangers.

If boundaries are the imaginary fences we place around ourselves to protect our own time, energy, and peace, we must do the work to identify what those boundaries even are. Imagine a circle around yourself. Within the circle are things you cherish, things that bring you joy and happiness. Outside of the circle are your stressors. People or things that may be getting in the way of your peace. Identify them. By outlining our limitations and triggers, we effectively allow ourselves to move to the next step, thus communicating our expectations to those around us. This is where many of us fail. We assume that others simply know our boundaries without them being communicated, or we're too afraid to voice them for fear of confrontation, but boundaries are essential in defining our relationships. Sure, not everyone will respect them. Some individuals will require us to reiterate the boundary over and over again until it becomes learned. Others will reject this new you altogether. In some instances, it may even require us to walk away from someone we know or love. It's okay.

The point is, you are more aware of what you need. When you are, you can better protect your space and your peace. Don't be afraid to set hard boundaries around things that are non-negotiable, and more importantly, don't shy away from working on the boundaries that are softer in nature, because those matter too. You won't always get it right, but if we communicate our request and stick to a consequence, we begin to lay the framework around a life we love instead of one we dread or feel unheard in. Who are you giving power to today? Make sure it's you.

~~~~~~~~~~~~~~~~~~~~~~~~~~~~~~~~~~~~~~

MOVING FORWARD

What boundaries are most important to you? Are there specific areas of your life that are lacking?

Who do you need to set boundaries with? List them here.

Now that you have identified what boundaries are most important and with whom they need to be set, ask yourself why you may be avoiding setting them. For example, are you afraid of conflict, do you feel guilty, are you being too accommodating, or wanting to please others?

How can you better protect your boundaries? Think of a few key phrases you can say in response next time it comes up. How might the individual react when you communicate this boundary?

As women, our boundaries are nonexistent, and this oftentimes has a large impact on our energy. What boundaries can you practice to better protect your energy and let others know what they are?

~~~~~~~~~~~~~~~~~~~~~~~~~~~~~~~~~~~~~~

Chapter 14

Battlefield

Failure Belief: My body is failing me

I remember sitting in the waiting room, a bundle of nerves. Excited, but also anxious to see the tiny bean growing inside of me for the first time. I couldn't believe it was all really happening. I was going to be a mother.

"Jennifer," the nurse's voice echoed over the waiting room TV as she propped the door open with her foot.

"That's us," I said to my husband, flashing a grin and a wink. "Are you ready for this?"

As we made our way to the sonographer's room, the technician dimmed the lights and handed me a gown.

"Go ahead and get undressed, and I'll be back in a few minutes."

I quickly shed my clothes and made my way to the examining table where I sat for a few minutes, dangling my feet and staring at the wall. Small talk seemed awkward at this moment, so I said a silent prayer to myself to fill the void.

"All set?" she said, knocking on the door. She dimmed the lights a bit more and turned on the monitor. "Is this your first?" she asked while getting everything ready.

"It is, yes," I said, managing to smile while nervously staring at the screen.

"So, here is the gestational sac," she said, zooming in with a few taps of her keyboard. "And you can see baby there, measuring about seven weeks." Her face went absent of all emotion as she began moving the wand from side to side. I waited for the audio to kick in so I could hear the reassurance I needed, but I wasn't going to get it today.

"I'm sorry, but I'm not finding a heartbeat."

I wanted to scream in her face. You're wrong. You don't know what you're doing. It's right there. My baby is right there on the screen. Just give me the thing. Let me do it. I'll show you. I can find it. My baby isn't dead.

But it was. As I sat there numb, tears streaming down my face, the technician put away the transducer wand and walked out the door. That was it. No condolence. No offering of remorse or additional words of I'm sorry. Just gone. It felt cold. How could someone be so harsh in a moment like this? Did she not have feelings at all?

I looked over at my husband from the examining table. "I'm so sorry," I said, bursting into sobs. He was pale, and his eyes bloodshot. We were devastated. Heartbroken and angry. Just then the door opened and we were asked to move to a regular exam room where my ob/gyn was waiting.

"Have a seat. I'm so sorry," she said, placing her hand on my knee. "Please know that what you are feeling is normal. Unfortunately, these things happen more often than you hear about. If you're up for it, I'd like to get you in for an additional sonogram today at the hospital to confirm what we're seeing. Their equipment is more advanced, and they can get a better look."

I nodded my head in agreement. "So, what do we do when the sono confirms what we already know?"

"In these instances we have three options. We refer to what you experienced as a silent miscarriage. When this happens, we can wait for your body to expel the baby naturally, give you medication to speed up the process, or order a surgical procedure we refer to as a D&C. The choice is yours."

As we packed up our things to head to the hospital, I made my way through the waiting room. It seemed as though every pregnant woman in the world had an appointment that day. I scanned the room through my tear-filled eyes and watched as they cradled their bellies and tended to their newborns. Their babies' coos were met with my mascara-stained face. Each woman, rocking their babies as I was yearning for mine. It all felt like a bad dream.

Once in the parking lot, I buried my head in my husband's arms and sobbed as we held one another—a full-body release of everything I had been holding onto. Every hope and dream. The anger and devastation. I knew in order to go forward I needed to be strong, but on the inside, I felt broken. I called my mom on the way to the hospital.

"Hi, sweetie," her voice echoed over my car speakers.

Tears instantly began streaming down my face.

"Mom..." I said, trying to form words over sobs.

"Honey, what's wrong? What happened?"

"I was planning on this all being a surprise. I was supposed to tell you that you're going to be a grandma, but we just left the doctor. There's no heartbeat. I'm on my way now to the hospital for another sono to confirm everything. I'm so sorry for calling you like this. I just needed to hear your voice."

"Oh, sweetie, I'm so sorry. I wish you had told me so I could be there. It's going to be okay. You'll get through this."

"Thanks, Mom. I love you."

The sonographer waiting area of the hospital was practically full, but I managed to find two seats near the back wall for my husband and me. I wrapped my arm through his as I stared at the blank tile floor. Numb. I didn't want to make eye contact with anyone. I didn't need their pity. I was angry. My body had betrayed me. As if that weren't enough, I was now sitting in a room surrounded by dozens of babies. Their mothers desperately attempted to entertain them until it was their turn to be called back. I resented every woman in that room, and I hated myself for it. I wondered if they knew. If they could sense my pain.

Why them? Why not me? What if I can never have a child of my own? What if my body is broken?

The sonogram confirmed what we already knew. I had lost my baby, and it wouldn't be the last. To make matters worse, my body failed to recognize the miscarriage. A surgical procedure would need to be ordered.

The night before my scheduled D&C, I began bleeding. I was warned that if done naturally contractions can happen with a miscarriage, but I don't know that anything could truly prepare me for what I was about to endure. I felt as though my insides were being torn apart. Instinctively, I got on all fours in an attempt to alleviate the pain. My moans quickly turned to growling screams as my entire body began tensing up from the contractions. How could something so tiny be this excruciating? My husband watched in horror, completely helpless to the pain my body was experiencing. There was nothing he could do.

"Should I call the doctor?" he asked nervously.

"No, I can do this," I said, gritting my teeth. "I have to." Just then, I felt the most intense surge in my uterus as it contracted in an attempt to expel my unviable pregnancy. My body was finally recognizing that something was wrong. I let out a scream and then lay on the floor covered in sweat. My husband immediately grabbed his cell phone and called my ob/gyn.

"Jennifer, your husband says you're bleeding," the night nurse's voice echoed over the speakerphone. "Can you describe to me what you're seeing?"

I wiped my face in an attempt to compose myself. "Um...there's a lot of dark blood, some clotting, and what looks like tissue. I'm supposed to be scheduled for a D&C tomorrow morning; can they even do that if I'm bleeding like this?"

"Yes. If your pain worsens or your bleeding intensifies, head to the ER. Otherwise, we will see you in the morning."

The anger I felt towards my own body was beyond my comprehension. Women are supposed to be life-givers, yet here I was on my hands and knees as my body failed to hold the life it had started. I felt betrayed. My swollen boobs and poochie stomach were reminders of what wasn't. The sense of loss that consumed me was overwhelming, not just for the loss of my baby but for a dream that may never become a reality.

I was broken. Devasted.

After the last contraction, the bleeding slowed and I was able to get some rest. I knew it wasn't enough. The next morning, I found myself waiting in the pre-op room for surgery. I wasn't sure what to expect, but I knew I was ready for it to all be over. The morning nurse popped in to check my vitals and ask me a few questions.

"How's the bleeding?"

"It's okay," I said, looking down at my stomach.

She handed me some paperwork about burial arrangements and upcoming memorial services, along with a silver medallion with the etched verse, "Safe in the arms of Jesus." I signed what needed to be signed, placing the pen down on the rolling table, looking away as I blinked the tears out of my eyes.

"You're handling this all very well," she said.

I didn't feel like it.

After the procedure, I felt hollow. I needed to heal, both physically and mentally. I knew the only way I could do that was to let go of the fear that consumed me. I would have to push past the anger and resentment I felt towards my body and my experience and shift my focus. I needed to see my body not for what it was incapable of, but for what it had endured. The ability to create and hold a life inside of you is a miracle so many of us take for granted. I know I did. We assume our bodies will always work for us, instead of against us. We believe our fertility is a given, and yet it's not. None of it is.

I spent the next few months healing from the inside out. I tried to give my body grace as my hormone levels slowly dropped back to normal. I allowed myself permission to release the guilt I felt for not being able to carry my baby and accepted that there was nothing I could have done differently to change the outcome. That's not to say it wasn't hard, or without tears. There were days when I didn't want to get out of bed. The sight of a baby at Target made me want to curl up in the fetal position and cry. The yearning I felt to be a mother was magnified by one hundred after our loss. But it wasn't until I reached the point of acceptance that I was able to heal. Make no mistake, my acceptance didn't mean I was okay with what happened; it simply meant I was no longer in denial. I was moving through the stages of grief and slowly reaching the other side. I even joined a yoga studio where my mom and I practiced yoga three days a week. I looked forward to the stillness. Moments where I would breathe slowly, listening to what my body needed and wanted.

During this journey of healing and forgiving myself, I realized that each and every day we wake up and take for granted that our bodies will just work. We don't notice or appreciate them for the miracles they truly are until we're ill or our bodies aren't working the way we want them to. We get angry and resentful while fighting feelings of brokenness. Believe me, I know. It took a long time to be at peace with myself and all my body has been through. To understand that my worth is not determined by the sum of my losses or the number of scars I hide. My body tells a story, and it's one we carry together. A story of heartache, healing, and learning to love myself as I am today. Yours tells a story too.

Maybe right now, you're going through your own loss. Maybe you're battling PCOS and trying to lose weight, but your body is fighting against you every step of the way. Maybe you have an auto-immune disorder that no one can see. Maybe all the trouble you've been having with fatigue and pain has been labeled for you, but you're unsure how to live with the diagnosis of fibromyalgia. Maybe you find yourself on your twelfth round of IVF, praying this is the one that results in your rainbow baby. Maybe you're fighting for your health, as you battle a medical diagnosis you never saw coming. Whatever it is, it can be frustrating when we feel as though we have no control over what happens to our own bodies. But the reality is so much of what happens to and within us is beyond our control.

Relinquishing that control is something many of us struggle with. We think if we do all the things, eat the right foods, drink the water, get 10,000 steps a day, meditate, and take the right vitamins and supplements, surely our bodies will do what we want them to. We'll lose the weight, minimize our symptoms, get pregnant, or ease our aches and pains.

But then it doesn't pan out. Our body has other plans, and it all just seems wrong. I mean, shouldn't we have the ability to have some say or influence on what happens to our own bodies, especially when we do everything right?

I don't claim to be a math whiz, but doesn't $x + y = z$?

Why can't our bodies work in the same way? The truth is, when it comes to our health, it's not black and white.

Unfortunately for me, it didn't matter that I took my prenatal vitamins religiously, or that I swore off deli meat even before knowing I was pregnant. It was never within my control to save my pregnancy. Nothing I did or didn't do could have changed the outcome. As much as I thought I was controlling and helping my body by doing all the right things, sometimes it simply doesn't matter. Acceptance is a hard pill to swallow. We go through life believing we have control of our futures, and then out of the blue...bam. Something hits you that you never saw coming. Your life gets flipped upside down, and you find yourself asking, "Why me? Where did I go wrong? Why can't I fix this?"

When I was healing from our loss, I realized I had two choices. I could bottle the anger and resentment I had for my own body inside, continuing this never-ending cycle of brokenness, or I could lean into self-acceptance and release control. I could choose to love my body for where I was despite all of its imperfections, all of its failures and shortcomings, because this body was the same one that allowed me to experience joy. It afforded me the ability to laugh with my whole being and to go outside and feel the warmth of the sunshine as it hit my face.

The same can be said for you. It's this body, the one with endometriosis, cancer, or lupus. The one battling anxiety, heart disease, or uterine fibroids that takes you on adventures with your girl-friends. I know things are so much harder than you thought they would be. I get that there's a whole list of things we wish we could change. But your body, the same one that breathes life into your lungs, is what allows you to experience life and love, and for that, gratitude can be found.

My friend texted me the best analogy the other day when we were talking about this very topic. She said, "We shift from a place of blame, guilt, and failure when we relinquish our control and begin to recognize our bodies as the vehicle to get us through life. The realization and acceptance that our bodies are like cars takes the pressure off the idea that if we did something different we could have somehow fixed our body or prevented the outcome."

Our bodies are the vehicle that gets us through life. What a powerful statement. Maybe it all comes down to this: while we can't always control what happens to us, we can control the response within us. Give yourself time. Time to heal and to grieve. Whatever thing it is you're facing, know that you are not defined by your illness or experience. The joy you have is within you, and nothing can take that away.

~~~~~~~~~~~~~~~~~~~~~~~~~~~~~~~~~~~

MOVING FORWARD

If you are experiencing an illness or loss, what have you found most difficult? (Acceptance, grief, guilt, shame, blame, etc.)

When we are struggling, it can be hard to focus on what our body is doing well. Write down two things you are thankful for today that your body provides?

~~~~~~~~~~~~~~~~~~~~~~~~~~~~~~~~~~~

Chapter 15

Curveballs

Failure Belief: Life has to go as planned

I had it all planned out. I was going to have 2.5 kids and crush motherhood. It had been a tough journey, but we were finally here. Our rainbow baby was coming. As I sat in our birthing class, hand resting over my ever-growing belly, the instructor flipped to a slide titled, Birth Plan. Many of us were first-time moms, wide-eyed and naïve to the fact that labor rarely goes as planned. I glanced at my husband sitting next to me and gave him a wink. "Our birth plan is a healthy baby."

I was 34 years old. One year away from what society affectionately labels, "geriatric pregnancy." Aside from the morning sickness and general uncomfortableness, things seemed to be going smoothly. I was still going into the office five days a week, donning maternity dresses and high heels that made every one of my co-workers nervous. But, all things considered, I felt good.

A few women in the class were planning for natural births. Others were going in knowing they would be requesting an epidural immediately. As for me, I was on the fence.

It was Halloween. Eleven days before my estimated due date. I woke up and plugged in my straightener. Resting my hands against the bathroom counter to catch my breath, I glanced in the mirror. The nausea was bad this morning. I made my way to the toilet, trying desperately not to wake my husband as the dry heaves started. Today is going to be rough. As I made my way back to the sink, I threw my hair into a top knot and grabbed a wash rag. The cold water felt calming against my already warm forehead. I opened my makeup bag searching for the one necessity in life…concealer. The holy grail. The big Kahuna. How they can get all that magic into such a tiny bottle, I will never know. But whoever that person is, they deserve a presidential medal. The dark circles under my eyes from lack of sleep were on full display without it. I had officially reached the uncomfortable phase. The one that leaves most women restless and on the couch from lower back pain. I threw on a maternity dress and made my way to the car, making sure to grab my trusted melamine barf cup for the drive to work.

I was proud of myself for making it my entire pregnancy while still going to the office. Sure, I had to elevate my feet on an upside-down trash can and a pillow to keep from forming cankles, but I was doing it.

"I feel off today," I told my friend as I opened up my cubicle cabinet, placing my laptop bag inside.

"You should have just stayed home," she said. "I swear if you go into labor and I have to drive you to the hospital, I'm going to lose it. You're giving us all anxiety."

"I'll be fine. Stop worrying."

Around 11:00 a.m., the cold sweats started in. I had an ache on my right side that came out of nowhere, and nothing was stopping the nausea. I felt clammy and awful. What was going on? A quick Google search had me labeled as near-death or appendicitis. Tack on the fact that I was nine months pregnant, and it could be a whole slew of other things. Regardless, I needed to go home.

I headed into my boss's office to tell her I was leaving for the day.

"Jenn, are you sure you don't want one of us to drive you home or to the hospital?" she asked. "Look at you. You're pale and sweating. I don't know that I feel comfortable with you driving on your own. At least have your husband come get you."

"I'll be fine. He's 30 minutes away," I said, fighting back nausea. "I'll be home faster if I just go now. I think I just need to lie down for a bit."

On the drive home, I cranked the air conditioning like a woman going through menopause, yet the sweat kept dripping down my face. My trusted melamine cup was getting a run for its money, and I never realized how far I lived from the city. I'm not going to lie; seeing that garage door open felt a little like paradise. As I made my way into the house, I headed straight for the shower. Everything hurt. I felt weak and light-headed. Omg, why does my side hurt so freaking bad? There was zero mention of this crap in the birthing class.

After my shower, I lay in bed, attempting to calm the nausea. Unfortunately, nothing was bringing relief and the contractions were starting in. My husband decided I needed to eat something, so he made me some chicken noodle soup. It was good for about five minutes. Until it wasn't. I couldn't keep anything down. The contractions were now three minutes apart. After a phone call to the hospital, they advised us to come in. It appeared to be time.

Once there, we were admitted into an ER room where they monitored my contractions for a few hours. Unfortunately, they weren't getting any closer together and I was only dilated to a one. If you've been in labor, you know that this usually leads to one thing...being sent home. I cringed at the idea of being 25 minutes away. There was something wrong. I knew it. My baby knew it. I couldn't leave.

Correction. I wasn't leaving.

I'm stubborn to a fault, but in this case it was my saving grace. I was admitted to the delivery floor where they continued to monitor my contractions and check my dilation for the next 24 hours. During that time, they decided to break my water and administer Pitocin to speed things along. Still, there was no progress. I was only dilated to 1.5 centimeters, yet the contractions grew more intense. I moved around the room from the shower, to the birthing ball, to all fours, and back again in an effort to ease some of the pain. Nothing was bringing relief.

Around 6:30 p.m. on November 1, I felt a contraction followed by the worst pain I've ever experienced in my life. As I cried out I held my belly, feeling for my baby. He had shifted all the way to the left side. The right side of my stomach was visibly flat. I clung to the bed rail as I begged my husband to help me. I thought I was dying. My body began convulsing as I shook from the pain.

The night nurse on duty came in, attempting to convince me this was all part of the birthing process and it was simply a contraction. Apparently, I was just a tired mother-to-be who couldn't handle pain. I completely lost it.

Full transparency, I had warned my husband on multiple occasions that I accept zero responsibility for what may come out of my mouth during labor. Don't get me wrong, I love Jesus, but I cuss a little. We had a bet going on whether or not any F-bombs would fly. Turns out, I was about to win.

"Listen to me!" I yelled. "There is something fucking wrong with me. I want a fucking doctor in here right fucking now!!!"

The nurse remained speechless for a moment, her eyes large as saucers as she looked at me with concern. "I'll be right back."

Within a few seconds, the doors swung open as a slew of nurses and on-call doctors swarmed the room. The cussing worked. I had gotten their attention, finally. I begged for an epidural or something to help deaden the pain as I tried desperately to unclench my fist so the nurse could draw my blood.

"The doctor is on her way," the nurse said. "We'll make some decisions from there. In the meantime, I'm sending this down to the anesthesiologist so we're prepped and ready for an epidural."

When the results came back, my white blood cell counts were through the roof. Clearly, I'm no doctor, but apparently, elevated numbers indicate an infection is present somewhere within the body. Concerned about what he was seeing, the anesthesiologist requested a second blood draw—an act that may have saved my life, and my son's. The results came back the same. Something was wrong.

When the doctor arrived, she informed me I had an infection. Therefore, they were moving to an emergency C-section. They were fairly certain that my appendix had ruptured which was bad news for both me and baby. Once in the OR, nurses held me upright to keep my tremors down long enough so the anesthesiologist could administer the epidural. My entire body was convulsing uncontrollably from shock.

I don't remember much after that, except for the tugging and pulling as the doctor pulled our nine-pound baby out. I got to see my son's face for a moment before the dry heaves and convulsions began again. At that point, I was put under completely while they worked to give me a full appendectomy and clean up my insides. Infection was everywhere. The pain I experienced was from my appendix rupturing.

Luckily my son was healthy and safe. I, on the other hand, was not out of the woods. After surgery, I formed an ileus in my stomach. I spent the next nine days in the hospital with an NG tube pumping all the remaining infection out of my body. Nothing about this birthing experience was what I had envisioned. Sure, I knew it would be hard, but this? This was a whole different level. I struggled to breastfeed because I couldn't eat. My son spent most of those nine days in the nursery so I could focus on getting well myself.

I felt like a failure.

During a time when my baby needed me most, I wasn't there. I physically couldn't be. I couldn't produce what he needed. I couldn't comfort him when he was crying. I couldn't bond with him and change his diapers. My voice, the one constant he had heard for nine months, was being replaced with those of strangers. He should be seeing my face and feeling my arms holding him close, but I couldn't. I couldn't walk down to the nursery and peek in the window to see him snug as a bug.

The guilt I felt was insurmountable.

To this day I don't even remember the first time I held my own son. I was so doped up on pain meds and recovering from anesthesia that I have zero recollection of that moment. It was supposed to be one of the most joy-filled times of my life, and I can't think back to it. Sure, I have a photo my mom snapped of the three of us, but in my mind, it's void. Void of a memory.

I don't know that I'll ever get over that.

For the first few months, I felt disconnected and unsure of myself as a mom. I had relied so heavily on others to care for him that I questioned my own abilities and instincts to do the same. I grappled with anxiety as my husband went back to work. Could I do this on my own? What if I failed? What if we don't bond the way we should?

Thankfully I have an amazing momma and friends who checked on me daily, one of whom dropped everything to be there for me for a few hours a couple times a week. She stood in front of my kitchen sink and washed baby bottles without even asking. She brought over lasagna and sandwiches each time she came. She never made a big deal about it. She never made me feel like I was failing or that something was wrong. She was just there.

She saw me right where I was. Isn't that what we all need? To be seen? To know that no matter how messy or screwed up things may seem, we're okay. We're not stuck. This isn't a permanent feeling, and by the way, what we're feeling is normal. Life rarely goes as planned. It's full of twists, turns, and curveballs we never saw coming. One minute life is great. The next, it's all going to hell in a handbasket. Maybe it's an unexpected phone call, a left-hand turn at a red light you should have been paying closer attention to, a divorce you never saw coming, or an unwanted diagnosis. But whatever it is, know that what you're feeling is normal. Maybe right now, you're experiencing anxiousness, anger, confusion, anxiety, depression, or general fear. It's okay. Allow yourself space to process and to feel.

You can't change the things that are beyond your control, but when life sends you swirling, you do have one thing—a choice. A choice in how we respond and how we pick up the pieces and begin again. Oftentimes it's easy to head down a path of why me? We become victims of our circumstances and place blame where it shouldn't necessarily be. When truthfully, does it really matter why it happened? Can knowing somehow change the outcome?

The answer is no.

I know we all have a blueprint of what we hope our life will be. Things like college, being married with two kids, a two-story house with a white picket fence, a corner office manager, and traveling the world fill our life manuals. We work towards our dreams, naïve to the idea that life may have other plans. Then, we get the college degree or bust our butts to start up our own business, only to fail in two years. We're left feeling unfulfilled and hopeless because the blueprint we had in our heads doesn't match our reality. Ideas of failure swirl around as we grapple with how we will ever overcome it, but we will.

What you need is time. Time to process and heal. Time to let go of the guilt and feelings of inadequacy. In order to do that, it's imperative that you hold space for yourself to process all of the emotions. Once you've allowed yourself to feel all the feels, work to shift your perspective. I know it's not an easy thing to do, but our hardest obstacles often become our greatest triumphs. Life is full of disappointments. What we do with them is on us. We can give our disappointments power to keep us down, or we can choose to get back up.

That's the beauty of the hard stuff. It shows us what we're made of. It requires us to dig down deep. Deeper than we ever thought possible. It forces us to let go of all the shoulds we had in our heads and, instead, meet life where we are. Look at me. Motherhood started out nothing like I had planned, but honestly, it's better than I could have ever imagined. It made me stronger and more resilient. It shaped me into the woman I am today. It turns out there's beauty in pain. We just have to look hard enough. When we do, it reveals the fighter in us, so we're sure to come up swinging.

〰〰〰〰〰〰〰〰〰〰〰〰〰〰〰〰

MOVING FORWARD

We all have times in our lives when things don't go as planned and we lose control. How did you respond? Are you holding onto something you need to let go of?

We all have a choice in how we respond when life doesn't go as planned. How has your perspective shifted since navigating the change? What did you learn? How have you grown?

Despite life's challenges and disappointments, what is something you can be grateful for right now?

Chapter 16

S.O.S.

Failure Belief: I shouldn't need help

I am one in seven. I didn't want to talk about it for a long time. In fact, truthfully, I was in complete denial. The postpartum screening papers the doctors have you fill out before every postnatal checkup I lied on. I checked the box I knew they wanted to see. You know the questions: In the past seven days, have you cried, felt depressed, or easily agitated? Followed by the answers all marked, "rarely." The problem was it was a lie. I wasn't always happy. I couldn't tell you the last time I had truly laughed. The kind that bellows from deep within your belly, leaving you gasping for air as you cross your legs, praying you don't pee. I was crying at the end of date nights, completely overwhelmed by where I was falling short. I felt anxious and like a failure. My emotions were all over the place, and no matter how hard I tried, I couldn't fight my way out of it.

I chalked it up to motherhood and general postpartum hormonal fluctuations. I kept telling myself it would get better; after all, this was what I always wanted. I knew early on that I would continue to pursue my career while juggling motherhood. The constant fatigue and general feeling of being on edge must be me simply adjusting to it all. Screening after screening, I would openly deny what was staring me right in the face. It was bigger than I could imagine, yet I kept telling myself it was all in my head. As if some-how, if I could make it just a few more weeks, it would be over. I would crest over the hill of crazy town and be myself again. Except it didn't happen. Month after month, the waves would pull me back under. Soon my anxiousness turned to a lack of patience and general moodiness. I couldn't control my response to situations. I would cry one minute and be laughing the next. It was like an out-of-body experience.

Have you ever wanted to run away from yourself? I have, prob-ably on more occasions than I would like to admit. I couldn't stand the person I had become. I was short-tempered and easily flustered. Moody and emotional. And yet, I used to be so poised, happy, and vibrant. As I stared in the mirror, I felt like a shell of myself, un-recognizable from who I had become. Still, my pride got in the way. I swore it would never happen to me. It couldn't. It wouldn't. I was stronger than anything postpartum could throw my way. I was mentally fit and capable of withstanding the insurmountable pres-sure and life-altering experience.

But here I was, crumbling and falling apart at the seams.

Why was it so hard for my body and hormones to process what had happened? Why couldn't I bounce back and go back to normal like everyone else? What was wrong with me?

I needed help, but I was afraid to ask. I didn't want to admit something was wrong because saying those words out loud would mean I somehow failed. Even when, deep down, I knew this was far beyond my control. Women don't ask for help. We pull up our bootstraps and get the job done. It's who we're taught to be. As I sat on the floor, knees pulled tightly against my chest, the tears fell and the overwhelming feeling set in. I couldn't keep doing this.

I grabbed my phone and dialed my ob/gyn to make an appoint-ment.

A few days later, I left work and walked into their office. The giant yellow daisy wallpaper looked more obnoxious than it did in the past. My eyes quickly scanned the room donned with soon-to-be mothers. I felt uneasy. There's something about the gynecologist that makes everyone uncomfortable. I found a seat in the corner of the waiting room and began to fill out the postnatal form the front desk receptionist had given me, this time answering truthfully.

As I turned it in to the front desk, the receptionist glanced down at the clipboard and then back at me. "The nurse will be with you shortly," she said. I wondered if she knew and could sense my uneasiness.

A few minutes passed, and I entered the room. It seemed odd being here for something other than a pap smear. The stirrups were neatly tucked into the bed. The white paper was perfectly centered on the exam table. It felt colder than normal. I nervously grabbed my phone, wishing for better cell service to mindlessly scroll till the doctor came in. Unfortunately, I was in a black hole with little to no 3G network.

There was a light knock on the door as the doctor came in going through my paperwork. "What brings you in today, hun?" she said, looking over the frames of her glasses.

"I need help. My patience is non-existent, I'm crying constantly, and I can't stand how I feel."

She pulled out the brown swivel stool and leaned against the white counter, closing my folder. "You want to run away from yourself, don't you?" she said, placing one of her hands on my knee. "I get it. Sometimes you wake up and the sound of your husband breathing pisses you off. You have no explanation as to why. You're just angry."

Tears began falling from my face. I felt seen for the first time in a long time.

"What you're feeling is normal. Well, not normal in the sense that we want it to stay that way, but what you're experiencing has a name. It's not in your head. It's called PPMD or postpartum mood disorder, and we can help you get through it."

One sentence had the power to save me. For months I believed that asking for help would somehow make me look weak, but it was actually the opposite. It took courage to walk through that door and say those three words. It took strength to fight the narrative that we need to tough it out, and instead fight for our own mental well-being. You don't have to suffer in silence. You don't have to cope with the struggles you're facing. Because here's the thing: mental illness, PPMD, anxiety, OCD, depression, menopause, ADHD, whatever it is—it doesn't care who you are. Believe me, I know. You can sit there and say, *it will never happen to me*. I was one of those people, but it didn't care. It crept in slowly and stole my joy.

Maybe right now, you're struggling. Maybe you've been denying what's staring you right in the face, just like I was. **But** listen to me, you don't have to hide. There's help out there. You just have to ask. It's time we lift this veil of unwanted stigmatism that surrounds mental health, and instead, meet women where they are. This is far beyond hormones after pregnancy. Women all over the globe are experiencing an emotional crisis due to a lack of mental health support. We struggle with feelings of loneliness, anxiety, exhaustion, depression, and OCD, not to mention gender stereotypes, while attempting to juggle motherhood and work. The psychological weight of these expectations is impossible. Unfortunately, far too many of us are struggling in silence.

It's time to address the elephant in the room. We're battling a giant...a silent one. A mental health crisis is not just looming. It's here, knocking loudly at our doors. It's affecting our children. It's infiltrating our schools and workplaces, yet we don't talk about it. Why is that?

According to a recent data study by the United Nations, 1 billion people suffer from some form of mental disorder worldwide. How much higher does that number need to get before we begin to take things seriously? I refuse to sit back while society quietly dismisses this issue. Now is not the time to stay silent; it's time to get loud. Mental health must find a permanent place at the forefront of our conversations. It starts by eliminating the ecological gap so many countries experience regarding funding and availability of formal mental health care. It's time businesses and corporations put their money where their mouth is regarding work-life balance and start providing their employees with adequate mental health care options to support it.

I don't know about you, but I'm tired of working and living for a society that refuses to acknowledge the social realities of today's modern mother and woman. We need a system that works for us, not against us. This includes providing women with adequate maternity leave, equal pay, affordable, comprehensive mental health care options, and onsite childcare, necessary to survive. It requires us to acknowledge that women no longer work to simply provide additional income.

Over 11 million families today are raised by single-parent households, with over 79% being headed by single mothers, many of whom are considered below the poverty level due to minimum wage. Sister, we can analyze the data all day long. We can put together pie charts and conduct studies, but it will never change anything until we acknowledge the social challenges women face. It's going to take a cultural shift. One that recognizes that what worked in the past no longer meets the needs of women and families in today's modern world. Our mental health is suffering because we're drowning in expectations. Women simultaneously care for our households while working full-time jobs, advocating for our children, fighting against inequality, and upholding fundamental human rights. We're constantly putting out fires and running on fumes. Something has to give, and it ends up being our mental well-being.

So, what can we do? First, I don't claim to be a doctor. What worked for me may not work for you, but know that there are resources, natural solutions, and medical professionals out there who can help. You are not alone; more importantly, you don't have to suffer in silence. Secondly, don't be afraid to advocate for yourself. We can provide women with all the adequate screenings in the world, but at the end of the day, no one knows you better than *you*. Trust your gut. If something feels off, say something. Reach out to a trained professional. I know many women who have benefited from therapy. Thanks to technology, this can be done virtually in the comfort of your home or in person.

When it comes to the workplace, identify what you need, and then speak with your supervisor or local HR team. Be specific in outlining where your mental health is suffering, and ask for their support and suggestions. Perhaps you need family leave or a more flexible work schedule. Lastly, come prepared and ready to ask questions when meeting with your provider. Does this medication have any side effects you should be aware of? Can this be taken with your current medication list? What natural options are available if the suggested one doesn't work? Remember, we want to ensure the treatment offered is right for YOU. If you feel like you need to talk to someone or have thoughts of harming yourself, seek the resources below, because you are not alone. You just need to say three simple words.

** Call or text 1-833-9-HELP4MOMS (1-833-943-5746) to connect with counselors 24 hours a day, seven days a week. This hotline offers free, confidential mental health support for moms and their families before, during, and after pregnancy.

** If you have thoughts of suicide or emotional distress, call or text 988 to connect with a trained crisis counselor. The Crisis Lifeline provides 24-hour, confidential support to anyone in need.

MOVING FORWARD

Take this time to check in with yourself. How are you feeling?

How did you answer the question above? Did you identify any trouble sleeping, increased feelings of sadness, lack of energy, fatigue, change in diet or appetite, anger, etc.?

What actions can you take now to advocate for yourself?

Chapter 17

Wear the Dang Suit

Failure Belief: I'm defined by my body

I haven't had a thigh gap since the fourth grade. Well, except for that one time in college when I ate only salads and did a thousand ab roller sit-ups a day because I worked at a gym and had all the time in the world. But, let's be honest; times have changed. I'll never see that body again. Nope. She's a distant memory. A vague reminder of "the one time" when my metabolism was my friend and not my mortal enemy. Add in motherhood, age, a global pandemic, and working remotely, and let's just say my coping mechanism has been, well—food. Specifically, cookies.

Remember that scene from *Mean Girls* where Regina George is wearing sweatpants at lunch and her friends ask her why? She looks up from her food and says, "These sweatpants are all that fit me." That's me. Except for not sweatpants. Leggings. Preferably the high wasted kind that sucks you in in all the right places. Looking back, I probably should have found more healthy alternatives to my never-ending sweet tooth, minor depression, and excessive Martha Stewart bake-a-thons, but it made me feel good at the time. Not particularly my knees or my ever-growing butt, but in the moment, it felt right. I was eating my emotions and burying them down deep. It was working, just not in favor of my closet or current situation. You see, we had promised my son we would take him to the local lake once the temps became warm enough, and today was that day.

The last time we had been to the beach was two years ago in Michigan. I spent those days in the sun covered in a T-shirt and shorts. I hated the way I looked both in the mirror and in photos. Let's be honest; the last thing anyone wanted to see was me frolicking around the beach in a bathing suit. *Your arms look so huge. There is cellulite in places I didn't know it could exist. You said you would start exercising and eating better, yet here you are. Ugh. How embarrassing. You've really let yourself go. Suck in your stomach. You look four months pregnant and your baby is THREE.*

This was the internal narrative running on repeat through my head on any given day. The criticism and harsh thoughts I allowed to creep in and run amock were debilitating. They were hindering how I smiled in photos and what clothes I hid behind. I felt embarrassed and unworthy. I knew how I had gotten here, but looking in the mirror and seeing my body staring back at me felt like betrayal. I was a shell of myself. I fixated on the number inside of my jeans, vowing to fit in them soon, and when I didn't, I felt like a failure—a constant reminder of where I was versus where I wanted to be.

As I stared at the bathing suit on my bed, I wanted to curl up and hide. *Maybe I should just throw on a tank top and shorts like last time.* The irony was that I would have given anything to have the body I shunned three years ago. I was fifteen pounds lighter. Yet, I criticized and beat myself up over all the things I thought needed improving, only to find myself looking back now with lustrous eyes. As women, that's what we do, isn't it? We're our own worst critics. Never satisfied. Always tugging, pulling, filling, and injecting. Determined to look any way but the way we do right now.

"Mommy, are you coming?" my son yelled from downstairs.

"Yeah, I'll be there in just a minute!" As I opened the door to my armoire, ready to grab a pair of Nike running shorts and a tank, I stopped and turned back to the black one-piece sitting on the bed. The scale wasn't going down anytime soon. I could hide, or I could go all in. There were twenty-five thousand 4.5-star reviews on this swimsuit for a reason. It was time to see what all the fuss was about. I put on the swimsuit and a beach coverup and headed downstairs.

"Mommy! Oh, I wike that swimmin' suit. Are you ready to be a fishy with me?"

"Yeah, babe. I am." And with that, we loaded up the Jeep and headed to the lake. At forty years old, I decided I'd had enough. I was no longer willing to be a spectator in my life simply because my innermost critic said I was better on the sidelines.

Now maybe you're reading this thinking, Jenn, I love how I look. There isn't a thing I would change about myself, and for you, I say congrats. You've reached the pinnacle of self-love that I don't know I'll ever attain, but as for the rest of us...can you relate? Do you see yourself wrapped in these words?

As women, it's our innate nature to deflect compliments and dissect every ounce of our bodies. We're taught from an early age that girls are to be "cute." Cuteness naturally derives from how we look or what we're wearing. Our bodies become the fixture by which we're judged and deemed successful. We're inundated with magazines and news headlines featuring hourglass waistlines and the latest fad diets. Influencers fill our feeds with clothes from Abercrombie and Fitch donned by women in their late thirties. Their size-zero bodies and perfect blowouts leave us wiping the sleep from our eyes while wondering how they can even fit in those clothes. Maybe it's just us.

Maybe we're the only ones who delete family photos because of the weird double chin you get when you laugh too hard or the lazy eye that always shows up at the most inconvenient time, no matter how hard you try to open your eyes. Maybe it's just us that fixate on the tummy roll you can't get rid of or how your nose is crooked and leans to the left.

But it's not. Our society has become obsessed with perfection. We believe that only thin women succeed. Ones who somehow reverse in age and become more youthful, so we inject ourselves with fillers and Botox. We replace our boobs because we don't like how they look in clothes. We pinch and tuck. We buy the Spanx and fold in the little section of our tummies that hangs over our underwear. We suck fat from our stomachs and put it in our butts. We hide our freckles and contour our faces. We purchase the cream and utilize red light therapy because someone on the internet said we should. We beat ourselves up because we haven't lost the baby weight even though it's only been two weeks. We set standards no one can uphold, yet we chase them anyway. We hide our very essence in the quest for numbers. The number in our jeans. The digits we see on the scale. The size of our waistline. The count of gray hairs on our heads or the number of wrinkles on our faces. The grams of food we consume in a day. We measure everything.

Is it good to be healthy? Heck, yes. Am I promoting or giving you an excuse to eat garbage every day and never make good food choices? No. What I'm getting at is there is a fine line between being healthy and prioritizing yourself and being borderline obsessed with chasing the unattainable. If the thought of putting on a bathing suit and enjoying your own life makes you want to throw up, it's time to reevaluate.

I know we don't have control over what swirls around in the media or the latest crap being thrown our way, but we do have control over whether or not we listen. We control our internal narratives and the way we speak to ourselves when no one is around. We can choose to show ourselves self-love, not for where we hope to be, but where we are today. We can love our bodies as they are, for what they've been through and how they've carried us.

My friend recently sent me a TikTok video that said, "It's okay if your jeans from last year don't fit. You don't have to feel bad about yourself or try to squeeze into them. You can just buy a new pair of jeans in a bigger size that makes you feel good about yourself." She's right. It's all made up anyway—the numbers, the sizing, the gimmicks, all of it. Wear what makes you feel good. You don't have to try to be something you aren't. So you don't have a thigh gap, or your arms flap like chicken wings when you wave. It's okay. You're more than how you look. Look at me. Today I went to the beach, my thighs rubbing together as I walked, yet no one noticed. No one stared or pointed. No one cared.

Maybe that's the point. None of it's real. The body standards. The expectations. I mean, who decided what the threshold is we should all be living up to, anyway? I picture some random old guy sitting behind a curtain like in *The Wizard of Oz*. It's garbage. It's fake news.

From the day we were born, society has spoon-fed us this idea that we need to look and be a certain way to be valued, but it's a lie. The supremeness and beauty you're searching for already resides within you. That's the power move they don't want you to realize. You see, society doesn't profit when women accept themselves as they are. That would mean we don't need what they're selling. They benefit when we doubt our very essence and purchase their marketing campaigns, serums, and programs in an effort to earn our worth. The kicker is we buy it, and then what? We still feel embarrassment and hatred for our bodies for not being enough. By making us feel shameful in our bodies and minds, they inevitably keep us small. The game continues, and we unknowingly pass it on to the next generation. The only way this made-up social hierarchy falls is when we call bullshit. It crumbles when enough of us stand up and claim our wholeness.

Knowing the lie is simply not enough. We can't afford to sit back and be victims of circumstance. We must reject the system in its entirety. I recently listened to an episode on the *We Can Do Hard Things podcast* by Glennon Doyle called "What if You Loved Your Body?" The guest on the show was author and activist, Sonya Renee Taylor. Trust me when I tell you to stop what you are doing and listen to this episode. It will transform your thinking and expose the lie for everything it is. I must forewarn you; you may feel angry. I know I did. I felt anger for not seeing what was really happening right before my eyes. Anger for believing for so long that I needed to change in order to be worthy. Don't be ashamed for not knowing. Instead, use that anger to fuel you forward into a place of love and acceptance of yourself.

When asked to describe what she means when using the words radical self-love, Sonya says this: "Radical self-love is our sense of our inherent divinity, that enoughness that cannot be exchanged for some capitalist-made external reality."

Do you have radical self-love for yourself today, or have you bought into the lie? Make no mistake; this isn't something that will happen overnight. Undoing years of cultural conditioning takes work, but you can get there. By healing the wounds we've self-in-flicted and rejecting what society has imposed upon each of us, we can harness the power within ourselves. You don't have to walk around feeling ashamed for who you are, the shape of your body, or the color of your skin. You were not made to be a one size fits all. I don't care what society has told you. You don't need porcelain skin, curves for days, and a perfect pout lip to be worthy. You don't have to be thinner. You don't have to hide your curls by straightening your hair day after day. You don't need to laminate your eyebrows to accentuate your face. You just need to be YOU. The system works because we've allowed it to infiltrate every facet of our lives. This narrative that our enoughness somehow comes from being something other than ourselves has been told over and over until we believed it was our own.

Jen Hatmaker, author of *Fierce, Free, and Full of Fire*, nailed it in her chapter "I Am Strong in My Body," where she wrote:

> Every company has miraculously found The Thing—forget that their findings all contradict one another based on their own personal junk science. They have us by the throat. They know it. They know what levers to pull, so we will open our wallets to their quick fixes. What would have to happen for us to honor our bodies? What is the opposite approach from this toxic cycle of comparison, impossible standards, shame, and self-harm? What might it look like if a generation of women started celebrating their outsides on their insides? Is there a possible path from here to there? Because the chasm is wide, and who do we think is coming

to our aid? The diet industry? Hollywood? Fashion culture? The beauty enterprise? They have nothing to gain if women refuse to hate their bodies. They are not our allies, no matter how much they profess to love women. We represent two key words to them: dollar signs. Get it straight.

She's one thousand percent right. The truth that scares so many is when women everywhere awaken to our own wholeness. When we embrace our uniqueness and divinity in a way where we cannot be shaken. When we see the lie for what it is and we reject it with every fiber of our being. That's how this all stops; when we expose it and refuse to pass it on to the next generation. I get it. Unpacking all of this is hard. As I write this, I'm writing to myself and you. Why? Because I'm still working on loving myself and reframing my thinking to embrace a healthy, more attainable body image. But it's time. Time to let go of the shame, fear, and blame you and I place upon ourselves.

Your value is not tied to how you look (or don't). It's not found through the consumption of others. Everything you are searching for is already inside of you. Do you believe it? I hope so because the world needs more of it.

Put on the dang suit. Own it. All of it, and never, ever apologize for it.

~~~~~~~~~~~~~~~~~~~~~~~~~~~~~~~~~~~

MOVING FORWARD

What are the messages you hear and see that you believe?

Remember, you define what it means to be whole. Only you hold power to dictate what those expectations for yourself should be. Check in, are the standards you are setting yours or are they being shaped by society, social media, family, the patriarchy, etc.?

What is the internal dialogue you have with yourself? What self-sabotaging thoughts do you find yourself saying?

Is there a trauma and/or situation from your past that you've yet to confront that may be shaping your internal dialogue? If so, what steps can you take to work through it?

List out what you love about yourself and your body. Then, write a letter to yourself.

Chapter 18

White Picket Fences

Failure Belief: She's doing it better

Open up social media on any given day and scroll through your feed. What do you see? Pristinely clean homes with white linen couches that somehow never have stains. Floor-to-ceiling custom kitchen cabinets, with organized pantries, and a secret butler's kitchen for good measure. There are coordinated mommy and me outfits and bathing suits for their fifth beach vacation getaway. Quick weekend trips with the hubs in swanky Airbnb's. Sporting events and Susie with her spelling bee contest awards and five thousand dance trophies. And it all begs the question—where does it leave the rest of us?

We scroll through the latest adventures of people we've never met. We watch people head to their beach homes in Florida or jetset halfway across the country to New York for fashion week. While I know it's a "job," I can't help but wonder how many of us, are looking at those images, comparing. Listen, I get it. No one wants to share a picture of their child having a meltdown in the middle of the Target aisle, but it's not just social media. We compare everything, from within our families to our neighbors, best friends, and complete strangers. We compare our looks, jobs, careers, homes, bank accounts, clothes, and even our kids.

Sure, their kid made the honor roll and yours didn't, but maybe he's had to battle dyslexia and ADHD to get there. The mom in school drop-off who just pulled up behind you in a new SUV? She got it because she lost her van in the divorce and needed something roomier and safer to chauffer the kids around. The couple you think just bought a beach house in Florida so they can be snow-birds in the winter, you're wrong. They're actually doing it to be closer to their ailing parents. The mom, who shows up to baseball games looking like a model is actually hyper-focused on her health because she's battling an autoimmune disorder no one can see.

My point? We compare, yet we have no idea where they came from or what challenges they faced to get here. We have zero clue what their story is, but because we see a snapshot in time or an image on social media, we think we have it all figured out, right? Wrong. They say comparison is the thief of joy for a reason. I'm going to be really blunt here, but it needs to be said. It is absolutely impossible for you to enjoy your own life when you're looking through the lens of someone else's. Remember back in school when we'd try to sneak a peek at someone else's answer on a test? The same can be said here. Keep your eyes on your own freaking paper. Life is not race. She's not doing it better or faster than you. There's no timeline. You don't have to go to a four-year university directly after high school, graduate with honors, and immediately land a corporate gig where you're making six figures. You don't have to get married by the time you're twenty-five, have a certain job, or live in a particular neighborhood to enjoy life. There are no rules for how to live your life: only the ones you set for yourself.

Listen, if every time you open up social media it leaves you feel-ing like garbage—do something about it. You don't have to follow your racist relative or the neighbor across the street who is con-stantly arguing about politics. You don't have to follow size-zero influencers with perfectly tanned figures if you're having problems with body image right now. If your house is a trainwreck, and you're barely scraping by, maybe now isn't a good time to watch videos from moms who put together elaborate crafts and lunches. Think about it. Pay attention to what you're consuming and how it makes you feel. If you find yourself looking around at your life and yourself thinking of all the areas you're lacking, re-evaluate. It's entirely possible to unfollow them or step away from social media altogether. You can mute, block, or hide anyone who isn't filling your cup. Social media was designed as a tool to connect us, but if it's only making you feel disconnected from your own reality, it's time for a breakup.

Trust me, I'm speaking to myself here too. I'm as guilty as the rest of us. Heck, just the other day I sent a text to my friend with a screenshot of an influencer modeling bathing suits on Instagram. "Why can't I have a body like that? I swear, she hit the freaking DNA lottery. Who looks like that after having two kids? She's a literal model." Never mind the fact that she's six inches taller than I am. Of course, the unrealistic expectation that I would ever even have the slightest chance of looking like her is a unicorn myth, but still, I was envious.

In one of her Facebook Coffee Talks, Mel Robbins said it best: "Jealousy is not about the other person. It's a signal. If you are jealous, it's something about what they're *doing* or what they *have* that your heart is telling you to pay attention to."

That one stung, but she's right. I was envious because I'm working on loving my body and getting into shape. She had something I didn't have, and it wasn't the first time. I remember the feeling I would get when I saw one of my fellow writer friends announce they had signed a book deal. I was jealous. Sure, I was rooting for them on the outside, but on the inside, I thought to myself, *why them?* Comparison is one of the worst feelings in the world, but I felt that way because there was something inside of me wanting the same. I wanted to write my own book. The jealousy and comparison I was experiencing was my heart's signal to take action and do the freaking work.

For you, it may be someone taking a vacation because you're longing for a break yourself.

A co-worker getting a promotion because you keep getting overlooked.

A baby announcement because you're silently struggling to conceive.

A date night because it's been over a year since you've had time as a couple.

A weight loss before and after photo because you're struggling to love your own body.

Comparison reveals the true longing of our hearts. So, what do we do? Besides unfollowing anything and everything that drags us down on social media, there's still an entire world out there we can compare ourselves to. While we can't stop comparison from happening altogether, I have found a few easy steps that help me when I find myself heading down the comparison trap.

1. Compliment her – Hear me out. I genuinely believe that women could run the world. The problem is the world has pitted us against one another. Women see other women as competition. We judge, berate, and knock each other down at every opportunity we get. But imagine what would happen if, instead of competing and comparing, we linked arms and joined forces. Celebrating another woman's victories doesn't diminish your own.

    Just the other day, I found myself standing in line behind a woman I would guess to be in her mid-thirties. She looked like she had stepped out of an athleisure magazine for Lululemon. Perfect blowout, Nike tennis shoes, leggings, with a bod to boot, long sleeve top, puffer vest, and the belt bag I've been trying to rock for months but can never manage. I immediately started comparing, and then I caught myself. "I'm sorry," I said awkwardly. "I just had to tell you I love your outfit, and your hair is absolutely gorgeous." I instantly felt better. "Oh my gosh, thank you," the woman said with a smile. "You just made my day." A compliment in place of comparison allowed me space to celebrate another woman while not diminishing myself.

2. Remember your why – This may seem incredibly remedial, but it works. Take the influencer whose tiny, toned body was making me envious. When done right, social media has

the ability to motivate us, but in this instance, it deflated me. I had a choice. I could sulk in my own misery, shove a cookie in my mouth while silently judging her, or I could get to work. Remember, comparison reveals our truest longings. My desire is to be more healthy and fit, and I'm working on it. It's not a race. Her journey looks different than mine. I could use her image as motivation and fuel for my why, or I could unfollow her altogether. The choice was mine, and it's yours, too.

3. Be mindful of the words we say to ourselves – You've heard it time and time again, but it's true, the words we say to ourselves matter. Whether we want to admit it or not, there is an internal dialogue running in our minds every single day. Pay attention to yours. What is it telling you? Are the words you speak to yourself kind and nurturing, or are you silently bashing yourself at every turn? Turn your thoughts to things you can be grateful for. How can you love yourself for where you are today?

    The thing about comparison is there will always be someone—someone who is skinnier, prettier, or seemingly more successful. Their life will somehow look shinier or more put together than yours, but I'm done wasting energy on someone else's highlight reel. It's not reality. I don't know their journey, and neither do you, so I'm focusing my attention on my own. I'm choosing to stay in my lane and root for the woman beside me. After all, we don't win by crossing into someone else's lane. We win when we stay in our own. That's the journey.

MOVING FORWARD

Identify the things or people that trigger comparison for you. What areas do you find yourself feeling jealous or envious?

What is your response? How does your comparison impact you? (i.e.: overeat, binge TV, snap at the kids, resent your husband, etc.)

Remember, jealousy is revealing something we desire within ourselves. What is it saying to you?

The words we say to ourselves matter. Are you self-critical, or are you self-loving? Write a letter to yourself celebrating your successes and the unique value you bring.

~~~~~~

WHO WE ARE

Chapter 19

Differences Aren't Always a Bad Thing

Failure Belief: I'm just a square peg in a round hole

Growing up, I knew I was going to be a career woman. I loved everything about it—the work, the routine of it all, the fancy briefcase, polished suits, and A-line skirts. If there was anything I was made for, it was this. The *Sex and the City*? That was me. I envisioned myself being Carrie Bradshaw, independent and living life to the fullest.

I got my first real corporate job when I was 25. I remember seeing the escalators and thinking, *I made it!* Fresh out of college, I took the first job I could land: an administrative role. It turns out that having a degree doesn't always get you very far when you have little to no experience in the actual marketing world. Regardless, I swallowed my pride and was grateful I had my foot in the door.

Fast forward three months, it turns out managing someone else's calendar and fetching coffee wasn't all it was cracked up to be. Quite frankly, I was miserable, and if I'm being honest, I wasn't terribly good at it. But I plowed through day after day, doing the best I could.

I remember sitting down for my first review, nervous as all get out, sweating through my deodorant and the lining of my suit. My boss gave a chagrinned smile from across the table. "I hate to say this, Jenn, but I think you're just a square peg in a round hole. I'm going to enroll you in a time management class. Hopefully, this will help with some of your calendaring mishaps."

Okay, I wasn't shocked, but the words still stung. I was in over my head and I had zero clue what I was doing. The *fake it til you make it* motto everyone preaches was not working. I couldn't tell you what was said after that. I was numb. As I sat there fighting back the tears, all I could think about was how I could be failing at something so *simple*. When the meeting was over, I vowed to do better and excused myself to the restroom. I needed room to breathe. As the yellow 1970s stall door slammed shut, I leaned against the cold, beige tile of the bathroom wall and sobbed. It was only 9:00 a.m. I needed to pull it together. So, I did what any grown woman in my shoes would do...I wiped the mascara from my face, tucked in my blouse, straightened my skirt, and readied myself to power through the remainder of the day. But as I looked in the mirror, I couldn't help but notice that the woman staring back at me looked different. My head wasn't held quite as high, and my light was a little dimmer.

I moved on from there, taking another administrative role before landing within the actual marketing space. I'm happy to say that the second time around, I thrived. But those words stayed with me, hidden behind every success, whispering beneath every compliment, discrediting my worth.

Think about that: One phrase had the power to alter and warp my perception of myself in an instant. Throughout my 15-year career, even now as a working mom, I've carried around those thoughts. Success after that moment was never because I earned it or because I was qualified; it was because I got lucky. After all, I'm just a square peg in a round hole.

But since becoming a mother, I'm slowly learning to let go. I'm learning that perfection doesn't exist and that maybe, just maybe, I was never meant to fit in. Molds are confining and predictable. I like to color outside the lines. Not necessarily on paper, but in life,

I'm different. Up until a few years ago, I saw those differences as shortcomings or roadblocks, but with every passing year, I'm beginning to see them as gifts. I understand that others' ideals are impossible to uphold, and I don't have to adopt them as my own. What someone might view as a negative quality may very well serve you in some other capacity in another role, making you a perfect candidate elsewhere.

Maybe right now, you're where I was, carrying some judgment someone said or a memory of how someone made you feel. Maybe right now, you wonder why you don't quite fit in or when you will ever find the right job or the right group of mom friends. You wonder why your relatives don't quite understand you and treat you differently or disagree with your parenting style.

Maybe right now, you too feel like a square peg in a round hole.

But let me remind you that you weren't created to be in someone else's image or to fit someone else's ideals. Each of us is unique. We hold gifts and characteristics that make us tick. We have strengths and weaknesses. And it's those gifts that make you the person you are today.

You were never made to be perfect. You were made to be you.

I've been labeled many things in my lifetime. I've been called stuck-up and a bitch without ever having uttered a word. I've been judged for my appearance and told my eyeliner was obnoxious and my face needed to be fixed. I've had my credentials thrown out the window all because I'm a woman. I've been labeled unreliable simply because I'm a mother. I've been pushed down and unfriended, ignored and forgotten.

But none of that defines who I am. None of that determines my worthiness and place in this world unless, of course, I let it.

If I've learned anything since becoming a mother, it's this: Our words matter. Not just the ones we tell others but the ones we tell ourselves. The words we allow within us are the very words that shape us. If we're not careful, they can leave us wishing to try to be something we aren't and suppress the very things we are. Words have the power to confine us or the ability to set us free.

From the moment your feet hit the floor in the morning, an internal dialogue runs through your head every minute of the day. I know because sometimes mine screams so loudly that I can barely think. This voice loves to remind me of all the areas in which I'm lacking and everywhere I'm sucking and falling short. It loves to fixate on words like *failure* and *not enough*, sitting quietly on my shoulder, waiting to voice its opinion at the most inopportune times. But I'm learning to quiet that voice and instead feed the one that betters my soul. The one that believes as opposed to doubts. The one that focuses more on what makes me strong as a mother instead of where I fall short.

Some days are hard. Some days the doubt creeps in and steals the day. I start to sequester and feel less than, but I never believe it for too long because I know who I am. I am the daughter of a King, and I am uniquely made. And, my beautiful, powerful friend, so are you. Let's choose to train our thoughts to serve us, rather than letting them beat us down.

MOVING FORWARD

What scenario or words spoken to you at one point or another are holding you back from your full potential? Look at each one and ask yourself if that limitation is true. If it is, is it really a big deal? List out five traits that are your strengths. How best can you utilize them in the future?

Chapter 20

Land of the Lost

Failure Belief: I don't know who I am

I recently had a crisis, a mini meltdown of sorts. On a random Tuesday in July, I found myself completely lost while driving to Costco. Not from a navigational standpoint, believe me my Costco runs were plentiful, but a complete loss of purpose. The kind that leaves you questioning who you are and what the hell you're doing with your life.

I did the only thing I could think of at that moment. While driving down the road, I sent an S.O.S. voice memo to my friend. You know the kind I'm talking about; long-winded, come to my Ted talk, one-sided conversation.

"I need a pep talk," I confessed.

"I've never felt more lost than I do right now. Everything I have put into my career, all the time, effort, sweat, and tears...It's getting me nowhere. And my writing? That's at a standstill too. Nothing is moving forward. It's like I'm stuck in this perpetual cycle of failure. Why is it so hard to be confident in our own abilities? I know I have talents and gifts, but I keep questioning everything. All of these fears and doubts keep mounting up. Like, what if I don't make the right decision? What if what I think I'm capable of I'm actually not? What if I fail? What if things are at a standstill because I really am just not good enough? I just feel stuck. I need you to talk me down from the ledge because I want to quit everything right now."

Tell me I'm not alone in this. If we're being honest with one another, we've all been there at least once in our lives.

We live in a *now* culture. We want what we want, and not a minute later. The very idea of waiting for anything makes us cringe. Our anxiety heightens, and our breath becomes shallower. We race against time, wondering why things aren't happening sooner. The latte you just ordered or your career advancement that seems to be at a standstill. They promised to make you partner at the firm two years ago. Have they forgotten? The baby you've been praying for. The bigger house your family desperately needs. The list goes on and on.

Yet, it's this quest for instant gratification that has left us feeling empty in everything we do. We see progress not happening on our timeline or the way we envisioned things and we equate that to failure. As a result, doubt begins to creep in, and we find ourselves hostages to the unknown.

But, it's not that cut and dry.

Our society places so much emphasis on *what* we do. Our culture has become obsessed with glamorizing words like *hustle* and *more*. Success is no longer defined by who we are at our core but rather by what company we work for, the title that adorns our office door, or how much money we have in our bank accounts. *What* we have or *what* we can show for ourselves has become such a defining quality of our culture.

I know this because I'm guilty of it myself. Believe me, I've drank the Kool-Aid, and it left me nothing but broken.

As I sat in the Costco parking lot, tears streaming down my face, I thought: *How did I get here? How have I become so utterly lost? I thought I had it all figured out.*

A voice memo pinged on my phone. It was Sis. A five-minute lifeline with hard truth seeped in nothing but love.

"Your focus is off," she said.

"You've defined yourself in what you do instead of who you are. You've allowed your work to equate to your success. But your

LIFE is your purpose, and your job is just that, a job. It's a way to provide and afford you with the means necessary to live out your purpose. It's not a qualifying denominator to our character. It's not a definition of who we are or our inherent success."

Dang, if that's not what my soul needed to hear in that moment.

She's right. The name you make for yourself will never bring fulfillment. Sure, it's okay to seek and even want recognition for your good work. We all should expect to be respected. But when we turn our attention back to really curating and pouring into the life we have outside of work, we shift our focus from the *what* to the *who*. You. Your family. Your children and your friends. Your LIFE. That is your purpose.

In recognizing this, we make the best choices not for what we hope to obtain but rather for where we are now. The *what* no longer becomes the center of who we are and what we are worthy of. It no longer drives us forward, and we begin to feel free. Free to shift to the things we enjoy and love.

The problem is so many of us search for purpose through goals and tangible things we can hold. We hang our purpose on the *when* just like I did. We think *when* we get the shiny corner office, or are made partner at the firm. *When* we have this amount of money in the bank or drive this kind of car. *When* we're able to buy this house on this certain street, *then* we'll be fulfilled, but what ends up happening? We get the thing, reach the goal, and it feels good for a moment, and then we feel empty again. So, we chase something else, hoping to find fulfillment and purpose just around the corner, but it's a vicious, never-ending cycle. We walk around aimlessly, grasping at straws because we've blurred the lines between what the world tells us will fulfill us vs. what we truly desire.

But perhaps that's the best-kept secret of them all. It's what society wants you to believe. When we find fulfillment within ourselves, we aren't maxing out our credit cards on things we don't need because we understand external things will never bring us joy. Perfection and the quest for more loses its grip on us as we embrace our own authenticity. Achieving simply to achieve becomes a thing of the past.

In her book, *The Radical Awakening*, Dr. Shefali states, "A common belief is that our purpose is something that needs to be found. This is a lie. Our purpose is within us. It is a state of being. Instead of chasing things, places, or people, we need to sit still and go deep within to ask: Is who I am in alignment with my most natural self? Is what I'm doing right now a match for how I truly feel?"

So how do we know when our life is truly aligned with our purpose? So many books tout that they've found the key to unlocking our purpose through their growth mindset process, but I think sometimes we overcomplicate things. Purpose is simply aligning your life with your own values and beliefs. And it's those ideals that should guide you in every facet of your life. Every decision you make, every path you choose should be grounded in your core beliefs. You won't find yourself searching outward for fulfillment because you understand that everything you are looking for is within you. You no longer set goals to simply set them, but rather with intention, using them as the catalyst to drive your purpose forward. When we unlock our purpose, it opens the door to living a life of fulfillment and meaning.

In the article "Five Steps to Finding Your Purpose," written for *Psychology Today*, Dr. Tchiki Davis identifies five steps to help us get reacquainted with our purpose. I've listed them below for reference, along with my own commentary.

"Step #1: Find what drives you" – This one is huge. Knowing and understanding where our passions lie allows us to make decisions both personally and professionally that support our values and beliefs. For me, fighting for the betterment and rights of women is my driver. It's a problem I want to solve and an issue I want to raise. It's seen through my writing, in the topics I champion for women in the workplace, and even down to the non-profit efforts I support. For you, you may want to be more environmentally conscious, or you're passionate about minimizing the economic gaps for women and families. Maybe a life of peace is something you want to practice and do more of. Perhaps it's investing in your family and cultivating a life you love within your four walls. Maybe you believe in the importance of philanthropy work and want to back your local community. Perhaps it's bringing awareness to the homeless or the foster care system. Whatever it is, what drives you is your passion. It doesn't always have to be something flashy.

"Step #2: Find out what energizes you" – This is not to be confused with what drives you. If we want to avoid burnout, we need to understand what excites us. For example, you can be driven to champion for women's rights, but if you invest your efforts in all the wrong places, you can quickly find yourself ready to give up. Knowing what fills you up vs. what depletes you allows you to identify a solution that aligns with your drive and purpose. Non-profit work in the family sector is incredibly important to me. So much so I sit on the Board of Directors for our local crisis nursery.

I share this story not to raise myself up but to illustrate a real-life example of the importance of knowing what energizes us. I was passionate when I began volunteering in our local shelters countless years ago. Unfortunately, I quickly overcommitted myself and burnt out. I did too many things all at once. I volunteered and made connections at not just one non-profit but all of them. I knew I was driven to help in this space, but I hadn't identified what energized me. It turns out while I love volunteering, where I thrive is in bringing awareness and creating opportunities for others to get involved. Now everywhere I go, every group I am a part of, I use it to bring attention to issues I'm passionate about. Again, know what energizes you. It can be the difference between a life of fulfillment vs. burnout.

"Step #3: Find out what you are willing to sacrifice for" – Friends, I'm going to be really honest here. When you find your niche, you're like a dog with a bone. Writing for me is cathartic. It's something I can't get enough of. This book has consumed countless hours of my life researching, connecting dots, sharing stories, and analyzing hard topics with friends over endless voice memos. It's been complex and challenging, yet I wouldn't change it for one second. As I type this, books, papers, and notes are scattered across my desk. My hair is in a wet top knot and I look like a troll, but I could care less. I'm willing to sacrifice sleep and time to do what drives me because I'm in my wheelhouse. Does that make sense? What is the area you're willing to sacrifice a lot for? Maybe it's teaching, your research in clinical studies, advocating for the LGBTQ group, or painting. Whatever it is, that is your purpose—a space where sacrifice doesn't feel like a sacrifice.

"Step #4: Find out who you want to help" – Remember back in the day when we were taught to always know the who, what, where, when, why, and how when understanding the framework of a project? It turns out they were right; this project just happens to be your life purpose. No pressure. Now, right now, you may be saying, Jenn, I get it. I'm a therapist. I want to help my clients. I'm a doctor, whose purpose lies in getting my patients well, but that's a broad term. If we were to probe ourselves and ask the hard questions, I think there would be a specific set of individuals we want to help. Let's take it back to the therapist example. As a therapist specializing in family counseling, you see a wide range of clients. Do you want to help all of them? Sure, but when you dig into the question and peel back the layers, you find that helping adolescent children struggling with bullying is your absolute wheelhouse. You could do it every day of your life because it brings you fulfillment and happiness in helping kids find themselves.

"Step #5: Find out how you want to help" – There it is again, the stuff we learned in middle school coming full circle, the *how*. I don't mean to squash your dreams here, but remember, we can't save the world; especially if we are putting our time and energy into places that burn us out. We know this now from previous steps. Remember how I volunteered for everything under the sun in the non-profit space? My efforts weren't effective. Taking on all the things and filling our calendars doesn't mean we are fulfilling our purpose. It means we're spinning our wheels. Find the area you are most effective in and focus your efforts there. This is your how.

I think it's important to understand that our purpose is a journey. As humans, we are ever-evolving, which means our purpose will change with us as we change. This is why it's so important we do the work to understand who we are. By embracing your uniqueness, you open the door for life to happen for you, not to you. We begin to understand that in order to live out our purpose, we must take ownership of our lives by identifying our who, what, where, when, and how. Only then can we harness our *why* and make choices that align with our core values and beliefs. For far too long, our purpose has been identified through our successes, but remember, your purpose doesn't need to be something monumental. You don't need to save the world. If your purpose is simply to live a life of simplicity and peace, focus your energy there. There's no wrong way to do this.

Purpose will look different for each of us. What drives me may be cringeworthy for you. But it doesn't make either of us wrong. Your purpose exists now, in this very moment, when we live for the life we have today. You're not lost. She's in there. Find her.

MOVING FORWARD

When we think of purpose, it's easy to get overwhelmed. We think our purpose must be something monumental, but in actuality, it can be something as simple as valuing inner peace or creating family moments around the dinner table. Write down what purpose means to you.

It's easy to define ourselves through titles and objects, but who are you if all of that were stripped away? What drives you most? What are you passionate about? What brings you joy?

Now ask yourself, are my goals in alignment with my purposes, or are they simply being driven by what I hope to obtain or other's projected expectations of me rather than my core beliefs?

What limiting beliefs (i.e.: perfection, concerns of the future, past failures, etc.) do you need to let go of to become your most authentic
self?

~~~~~~

Chapter 21

Grace upon Grace

Failure Belief: I'm a bad friend

Count how many friends you have. Not from your sorority or high school days or the number of friends on your Facebook profile. I'm talking now. Today. How many do you consider your true friends? Your ride or die. Ones you could call on a moment's notice, and they would be there. Friends who know the real you. Every embarrassing story and all of the latest family drama, yet they still choose to love you anyway. For me, that current number is four. At certain times in my life, it's been one, five, three, and even zero.

Yes, you read that right. Zero.

Clearly, I'm the furthest thing from a friendship expert. Heck, up until a few months ago, I had never seen one of my best friends in real life, EVER. I know what you're thinking. Jenn, how can you have a best friend you've never seen? It's easy; the internet. We connected four years ago over writing and the rest is history. In my defense, we talked about seeing one another on multiple occasions, but thanks to a global pandemic, kids, and the fact that we live states away, it just never happened.

For the longest time, it was a running joke that we both had zero clue what our legs looked like. When the stars aligned and we were able to meet in Chicago, I honestly was a little nervous. For a brief moment, I caught myself worrying about whether or not I would live up to her expectations of me. Can you believe that? Me, a grown forty-year-old woman, still concerned about my own likeability, from a friend I'd known for four years, no less.

The good news is, she didn't run for the hills. With our arms in the air and our coffee flailing, we got out of our cars, screamed, and hugged one another. I guess that's what happens when you've been waiting four years to squeeze your person. Quite honestly, it was the best day and one I desperately needed. There were adventures at the museum and thirty-dollar stuffies from the aquarium that our kids didn't need. It was chaos, but the good kind. We walked nearly nine miles that day, but I didn't even really notice, and neither did the kids. They loved every minute together. Finally, around 5:00 p.m., we called it quits, buckled everyone in, and vowed to do it again soon. Soon is a relative term when you're juggling kids and life, but I guarantee we won't wait four years. At least, that's the goal, anyway.

If I'm being honest, friendships in motherhood are hard, but friendships as you age are even more complicated. I know I'm not alone in this thinking because so many of you have told me. Women everywhere are struggling to keep the friendships we do have, let alone form new ones. We cite a lack of time and energy as our reasoning for not having them. We push them aside instead of investing in them because it takes too much effort. Then what happens? We let them fizzle out and wonder if we're just not friendship material, but the real reason is—we lack trust. Sure, the time and energy thing is partially true, but we also fear our own likeability, so we choose isolation and loneliness over connection.

That one stung a little bit, didn't it? It's okay. It was meant to.

I do it, too. I mean, I just confessed I was worried that my friend of four years might not like me when she met me in real life. Really? What was she going to do, take one look at me, find me repulsive, pack up the kids, and leave? Come on. Why do we do this to ourselves? She has been my friend for four years. We've seen one another at our worst—top knot, no makeup, day four of unwashed hair, and crying kids in the background. We've coached one another through career moves, finances, organizational ideas, sleep training kids, and everything in between. There isn't anything she doesn't know already.

There's a meme I see shared frequently that says, "Adult friendships are just two people running into one another and saying, 'I haven't seen you in forever, we should really get together,' over and over until one of you dies."

It's laughable because it's true, but it's also incredibly disheartening. I get it; last-minute weekend getaways with the girls are a thing of the past. The impromptu coffee dates and happy hours after work that used to fill my calendar are now replaced by school activities and doctor appointments. Friendships at forty look a whole lot different than they did in my younger years. Ones that used to be based on face value are now seeped in vulnerability, with trust and rawness I never thought possible. We know the ins and outs of one another. We know our kiddos' birthdays. We know when one is sick or when something isn't right. We celebrate together and cry together. We cheer one another on with a fierceness that is unmatched.

Our friendships consist of lengthy voice memos that I listen intently to like podcasts, and random TikTok videos or Instagram memes that only we would understand. It's late-night rage texts and links to cute clothes we saw while mindlessly surfing the internet when we should have been sleeping.

It's sending a bottle of wine to celebrate a milestone only you know about.

It's laughing so hard you can't breathe (and you pee a little).

It's motivating one another to work out and eat better, knowing full well that in two days, we'll wonder why our pants don't fit as we order that sugar-filled Starbucks we need to survive.

It's a safe place to share our struggles and voice our fears without being judged.

It's knowing we're not alone, even on our hardest days.

My friend just called as I type this. She was on her way to a concert after traveling for work this past week. She simply called to check in. There was no agenda. No M.O. Just two friends going through life together, extending all the grace in the world for days gone by as we navigate life and friendship. It's been over a month since we last connected. Sure, that time is filled with voice memos, texts, and missed phone calls, but sometimes the other doesn't respond. We get busy. Life happens. The kids start screaming, and we forget to check in. That's okay. It doesn't make you a bad friend.

I know your Instagram is filled with women smiling for the camera, sandwiched between ten other girlfriends, traveling together with the words "friends forever." You wonder how on earth they can manage to have that many friends, let alone keep them forever, while you struggle to find or keep the ones you have, but you're not friending wrong.

I don't care what society has taught you about friendship. Life isn't a popularity contest you're simply not winning. You're not broken just because you lack an entourage of friends. Friendship is more than face value. It's about vulnerability.

I'm supposed to tell you my secret to creating lifelong friendships, but I think that's where we've gotten it wrong. Often times we get so caught up in this *friends forever* concept. We believe friendships should span decades and lifetimes, and when they don't, we feel like we failed. But friendships aren't always going to last forever. I don't know that they were ever meant to.

Have you ever found yourself staying in a friendship out of guilt or because of [insert reasoning here]? We can't pinpoint why or when it happened. All we know is things begin to feel different—the compatibility shifts. What once may have seemed effortless now seems forced and tense. Your shared interests now consist of only the past, yet we hang on to them out of obligation. Then what happens? We become resentful.

Listen, that's not an example of you being a bad friend. It's called life. If you're growing and evolving, your circle will change with you. Outgrowing a friendship doesn't mean that either of you failed. It just means you are on different paths. People will come into your life for seasons or perhaps mere moments. If we're lucky, some will last a lifetime, yet it's essential to understand that each is equally important. Every friendship serves a purpose and leaves an imprint on who we are today.

Friendships challenge us and make us a better person.

I recently listened to an episode of *The Mel Robbins Podcast* where she focused on friendship and why finding and keeping them as an adult is so dang hard. During her talk, Mel identified five lies we tell ourselves about friendship. Lie #3 was exactly what I just talked about. She calls it "The big misconception – BFF," but she also dissected four others worth noting.

Lie #1: Everyone else's life is a party except mine

Lie #2: People just don't like me

Lie #3: The big misconception – BFF

Lie #4: You need to be friends with everyone

Lie #5: I'm too busy, tired, [fill in the blank here]

Do you find yourself identifying with any of these? I know I do. But perhaps the biggest misconception that no one seems to be talking about is this idea that friendships should look identical to where you are in life.

My best friends span from their 20's to their late 50's. Some are single, some are mothers, and others are embarking on retirement. Yet each one of them brings such depth to my life. They challenge me to be a better person. They empower me to be bold and are there for me like family.

The point is, there is no magical number of friends that will make you feel whole. They don't need to look a certain way or do something specific. It simply takes one. One person vulnerable enough to meet you where you are. Someone who isn't afraid to openly show you their messy while embracing yours. One who provides you with the emotional and mental support you need, who roots for you and encourages your dreams.

Don't be afraid to put yourself out there. You're not a bad friend. Friendships require flexibility and a whole lot of grace. Grace and understanding that on the other side of the phone is a friend with an entire life and family of their own. Friendship is like marriage. It takes work. It takes intention and vulnerability. I get it. I know opening up to someone can be scary, but humanness in its truest form is what connects us. We have to start getting comfortable with being uncomfortable. After all, vulnerability is what allows us to feel seen and heard. Embrace it.

I took a thousand pictures that day in Chicago, one of which sits in my office next to a wooden sign that reads, "A sweet friendship refreshes the soul." Isn't that the truth? There's no denying friendships take work, but the meaning and purpose they bring to our lives are irreplaceable. You were never meant to live this life alone; you were built for connection. In a world hyper-focused on filters and changing the way we are, there is a sweet release in truly being known by someone. Friendships are the lifeline we didn't know we needed. They provide us with a safe place to share our broken and messy selves without fear or judgment. They call us on our bullshit and hold us to our goals. There's a peace that comes from truly being known.

So, while I may not have a posse or lifetime friends, I have something better—life*line* friends. Ones I could call on a moment's notice. Ones who know what I stand for and what makes me tick. Friends who understand what drives me insane and how to talk me off a ledge.

That's friendship. The voice you sometimes don't even know you need. The text that comes at just the right time. The *you got this* voice memo that reminds you of how strong you are. It's knowing that no matter what, you have them in your corner—always.

Here's to the friends that get us. Who serve up heaps of grace with their coffee and whose voice feels like home.

~~~~~~

MOVING FORWARD

When was the last time you checked in with your friends? Text your people or send a quick voice memo. It takes a few minutes to nurture our relationships and let others know we are thinking of them.

Time is often a resource many of us have little of. What are some ways you can capitalize on the time you do have together with friends? Things like grocery shopping or exercising with friends can be dual purpose.

If you find yourself struggling to make friends, what are some tangible ways you can take action to be more vulnerable and put yourself out there? (Don't be afraid to leverage your current social network or tap into your local community—book clubs, classes, etc.)

Are you holding onto a friendship that may no longer be serving you? Ask yourself this simple question: Is time spent with this person energizing or depleting me?

Identify five characteristics that make you a great friend.

Chapter 22

Get Out of Your Head

Failure Belief: I'm not qualified

I received word a few months ago that I would be getting an interview for a position that had been posted within our group. I felt as though the temperature in the room had gone up about fifteen degrees. With a billion thoughts swirling around in my head, I sent a voice memo to my friend, "How is it that something I have literally done for over a decade, and I know I'm more than qualified for, I somehow still don't feel qualified? Why do we do this to ourselves? What am I so afraid of?"

I knew the answer. I was scared of failing. I was afraid I would fail on a much larger scale than I ever would if I were to just stay small. When you stay small and you fail, no one notices. No one is there to point out the fact that you screwed up or to judge you. No one is telling you maybe you aren't the most qualified or that this isn't really your strong suit. No one sees it, but whenever you play big and you go for it people notice. They look for you to fail, and when you do, you're met with phrases like:

We gave her the opportunity. I guess she didn't want it bad enough.

She didn't step up.

She's just not qualified or ready.

She's not leadership material.

But I think it's deeper than just a fear of failing. This fear of failure is rooted in fear of rejection. As women, we place our value in our ability to be valuable to others. If I somehow fail as a mother, daughter, sibling, friend, or co-worker, it's not without consequence. I must not be bringing enough of myself to the table; therefore, I'm not valuable. So, we begin to doubt ourselves. We question and analyze everything. Am I taking on too much? Can I juggle being a mother, an author, a wife, a daughter, and a full-time professional? Can I add this to my plate without impacting something else?

Yet if this same opportunity were given to a man, he would never doubt himself. He would never question or think about failing because fear isn't the driver for men. They operate on confidence in their own abilities. Whether they have done something for five minutes or five years, they know how to make it happen, and if they don't, they'll learn. They aren't afraid to take it. They answer the question: *Why are you the best candidate for the job?* With, "If there's someone more qualified than I am, I encourage you to hire them."

Talk about a mic drop. I want that type of confidence in my life.

In an article for *Forbes* magazine, Nancy Frank stated, "Women aren't taking action often enough, and that's crucial. We don't have to be perfect. Men are confident about their ability at 60%, but women don't feel confident until they've checked off each item on the list. Think about the difference between 60% and 100%."

She's right. I needed my qualifications to match each and every line item. When they didn't, instead of submitting my resume at 75%, I sat there thinking of the fifty thousand reasons why I shouldn't go for it. I'd much prefer psycho-analyzing the implications of my actions and whether or not this decision will impact x, y, and z. Because let's be honest, there's no plausible way I am as qualified as people think I am. I'll only be letting them down.

"So, what do you think? Are you ready to crush it?" my husband asked, entering the office.

"I don't know. It's going to require me to interact with a lot of high-up people at the company. What if I say something stupid? You know how I black out sometimes when I'm talking. I don't know if it's a good idea to go for this, with everything else I have going on."

"You've sat here and complained about not getting opportunities, and now that you have one, you're not going for it. If you don't take this and show up like the qualified woman you are, that's on you. But I don't want to hear any more complaining."

Oof. He was right. It's what I was doing. Truthfully, it was easier to sit back and complain about why I wasn't getting the opportunity because I'd become complacent. I was comfortable where Corporate America had labeled me. I was okay playing small. Going for it would mean leaving it all on the table and going big. It would take me going outside my comfort zone, embracing change and the unknown. It meant I would actually have to walk the talk I preach to women every day.

You see, openly denying what you're more than qualified for is like denying your own self-worth. You're literally saying out loud: *I'm not worthy*. I get it. Part of fear is the unknown. It's in change and the implications of what that change can bring, but I'm tired of carrying around the weight of the words I'm not [fill in the blank here].

So, you didn't make the cut or get the job.

So, you didn't get into the school you wanted.

Or maybe you got passed up on a promotion or an opportunity.

So, you haven't lost weight, or the number isn't quite where you want it to be.

So, you didn't make the lead chair in the orchestra, or maybe your business loan fell through.

Whatever it is, for the love of everything, don't you dare sit down. I don't care if someone told you that you can't or shouldn't. We have to shift the narrative in our heads because life is full of rejections. Look at legendary *Vogue* editor-in-chief, Anna Wintour.

In 1975, she was fired from her junior editor position at *Harper's Bazaar* for her fashion edge, only to become one of the most successful women in the fashion industry.

When asked about failure she said, "Everyone should be sacked at least once in their career because perfection doesn't exist. It's important to have setbacks because that is the reality of life."

We have to get past this idea that we're somehow better off by undermining our own abilities. We're not. Fear of failure is paralyzing women everywhere. It's causing us to sit back quietly as we continually steamroll over our own credentials, but how do we overcome it?

Caroline Castrillon, a writer for *Forbes* magazine, lays it out in three easy steps (commentary is my own):

1. "Identify the source" – This is about putting a name to your fears. What are you afraid of? Is it disappointing someone? Fear of rejection or disapproval? Are you afraid you'll job fail and lose your job? Do you fear change or the unknown? Are you afraid you'll be in over your head? Whatever it is, knowing and naming the source of your fears is half the battle. For me, I was afraid I would be in over my head. I was worried I'd get the job and then disappoint everyone around me by somehow not measuring up.

2. "Visualize Obstacles" – There's something to be said about anticipating your hurdles. When we have a plan and are aware of things that may get in the way, we feel better equipped to handle them. By allowing ourselves to look towards the future, we create a strategy around what to do, when, and through actionable steps. I call this "scenario mapping." Yes, I totally just made that phrase up, but go with it. Let's say, like me, you're applying for a job. What's the worst-case scenario here? You won't get offered the job, right...then what? Do we apply for others? Start looking outside the company? Map out how that result impacts your next decision. On the flip side, let's say

you do get an offer. What does that look like for you? How can you ensure your success? Is there a training you can pick up or someone you could contact to help mentor you?

3. "Adopt a growth mindset" – If I had a dollar for every time I heard this phrase thrown around at work, I'd be rich, but hear me out. I know the words are cringeworthy, but it really comes down to this: Understanding that when we fail, there is always a tangible takeaway. What did you learn? How can you use a particular failure to propel you forward?

By identifying our fears and mapping out the possibilities, we equip ourselves to be better prepared for our future. This idea that failure isn't an option is a lie. It's not a matter of 'if' you fail, but 'when.' Failure is always a possibility if you are taking chances and willing to embrace risk, but it's what you do with it that determines where you will land.

If you want to start your own business, get off your butt and apply for the dang loan.

If you want to run a marathon, start training and do it.

If you are up for a promotion, stop telling yourself all the ways you aren't qualified and start advocating for yourself instead.

If you are speaking to someone, speak confidently and look them in the eye.

Stop letting fear get in the way of your dreams. After all, our minds have this uncanny ability to produce what we feed them. Do you want to tell yourself you can't? Well then, quite frankly, you won't. But when you flip the script and tell yourself you can, something amazing happens. You will. Sure, you might fail, but you no longer see failure as the opposite of success but rather as a part of it.

I understand now that failure is not a sign of our inadequacy or lack of qualifications. It's a sign that you're taking steps forward. Use your failure as fuel to propel you into the future you.

Pause. Reflect and keep showing up. Each time, better equipped to shed our preconceived notions of ourselves and silence the noise. After all, all we can do is bring our whole selves. Maybe it's enough for the job or the thing you're pursuing. Maybe it's not.

For me, today, it wasn't enough. I just received a call saying another candidate was selected for the position. Someone with a more technical background than I offered. A slow visceral gut punch I unfortunately anticipated but wasn't quite mentally prepared for. I knew the risks. I weighed the possible outcomes and decided that my qualifications were just as good as anyone else's, so I went for it. I left it all on the table, and you should, too.

Remember, no one can tell you when to quit, at least not if you don't allow it. Trust me when I tell you, you're not alone. There is an army of women standing right alongside you. We've heard the words "no" and "you can't" time and time again. We've internalized them and questioned every ounce of our abilities, but today we start by naming our fears and replacing the words *I'm not* with *I can* because we understand that our value is inherent even when we're not 100% qualified.

Don't be the woman that was too afraid to go for it.

After all, we've got glass ceilings to shatter and rooms to fill, and we can't do it by remaining seated and playing small.

MOVING FORWARD

In what ways have the words "I'm not" held you back in your life?

What is something you would pursue if you couldn't fail? What dreams or tasks have you pushed aside out of fear of failure?

What is holding you back from going after that goal? Name your fear. Are you afraid of the activity or the outcome?

Identify the obstacles that could happen if you try.

What happens if you do nothing? Would you be happy?

Write two I CAN statements that empower you.

Chapter 23

Inherent Value

Failure Belief: I'm not worthy enough

I was recently asked in an interview to describe a time when I had to stand up for something I valued. In the corporate world, they were waiting for some politically correct answer that focused on a situation in the workplace, but what I provided them was something they weren't expecting. I answered with this:

"You're looking for a concrete example, but I would argue as a woman and mother we stand up for our value every single day. We can't afford a day of rest, or we lose. We lose the fight to have our voices heard, our opinions valued, and to be where decisions are made. Standing up for something you believe in isn't a one-time deal; it's a journey. We fight for a seat at the table every day, not just for ourselves but for the future—for our daughters and granddaughters. But to answer your question, beyond that, I recently fought for myself. I stood up for my value, my worth, and what I know I am capable and deserving of. I asked for a promotion."

There was a long pause on the other end.

"I can honestly say I've never had that question answered like that. But as a woman, I relate to every word," she said. "The road has not been easy."

Sure, I could have given them the answer they were looking for. I could have checked the box and moved on to the next interview question hoping to get to the next round, but if that next step comes at the cost of speaking my truth, I'm no longer interested.

As women, we wait. We think, if only. If only we can shoulder a bit more of the burden, if we can take on a little more responsibility, stay the extra hour, be a certain way, do more around the house after the kids go to bed, *maybe* someone will notice. *Maybe* someone will deem us worthy and see the value we bring.

But your worth is not defined by your output. You can't produce worthiness. Why? Because you are worthy today as you are. Yet we still use phrases like:

It would be nice if I could get a raise.

I'd like to have a promotion.

I wish I could start my own business.

Do you hear the hesitation in these asks? Do you sense the lack of confidence in your self-worth? Phrases like these place our fate in someone else's hands. It's as if we took our value, our self-worth, slapped it on a platter, and handed it to someone else to decide if we are worthy enough.

But, hear me. Your worth is inherent. It's unchanging and unmovable. It exists no matter what. You can't create worthiness. You can't manifest greater worth than you are today.

Your value exists in the here and now, but it's up to us to unlock and take hold of our intrinsic value. When we believe in ourselves, our dreams, and our potential, not for what others see, but for the self-worth and self-value we know we deserve.

After all, Mel Robbins said it best when she said, "No one is coming."

No one is coming to give you that promotion.

No one is coming to save your marriage.

No one is coming to help you reach your goal.

The power resides in you.

She's right. How can we expect others to value us when we don't even see the value in ourselves? How can we expect others to find us worthy when we feel unworthy every day? How can we expect others to fight for us when we sit back and refuse to fight for ourselves?

This goes far beyond finding a seat at the table, fighting for your salary, or how much society does or doesn't seem to deem you worthy. This is about valuing yourself as an individual. Every piece of you, every imperfection, everything that manifests inside of you that makes you who you are today. Everything that drives you forward, with every passion and desire. It's loving your whole self, not just the bits and pieces you pick apart and choose to love. It's valuing yourself enough to say in any instance, I am worthy I matter, whether that's in your marriage, your friendships, the workplace, or in the church.

I am worthy because I know the value within myself.

It's a powerful statement, isn't it? One that has the ability to transform how we see ourselves and our future. A statement that reminds us no matter what today looked like, regardless of where you are in this moment or what you had to do to get here- *you matter*. Do you believe it? Are you projecting that confidence you feel within yourself outward toward others, or are you hiding? Waiting for someone to notice and tell you you're worthy. If you answered the latter, I can tell you from experience you'll be waiting your whole life because no one is coming.

It wasn't until I fought for myself that others took note and started to listen. They realized I was no longer complacent about accepting the fate *they* gave me. I now held the keys to my own value, and if that value was not reciprocated, I was just fine in finding it elsewhere. Not everyone will see your worth, and that's okay. It's not your responsibility to make them see it. It is, however, your responsibility to see it within yourself and stop undermining everything you do.

In her book, *Fierce, Free, and Full of Fire*, Jen Hatmaker wrote:

Listen, there is nothing wrong with how much space you are geared to take up. There is not a superior way to be, regardless of what messages you are picking up in the atmosphere. You do not need to be more or less; what matters is decoding what container you flourish in. This is your work, your verdict, and your line to hold. It is upon you to insist on your space, even when it is discouraged or belittled. When the command aimed at women is "be less," the tactics include insulting, condescending, bullying, and manipulating. The goal is to make you shrink, so the maneuver will attempt to make you feel small. Your competence will be challenged, your authority dismissed, your experience questioned, your voice silenced. The endgame is your feeling deflated enough to bench yourself. Happens all the time. This coercion can occur inside a marriage, extended family, career, church, friendship, or any community. With women having already internalized a lifetime of messages that they are too much, it doesn't take much browbeating to reinforce the memo. You are not required to justify your space nor hustle for approval. If someone wants you to be smaller, that is their problem.

She's right. Placing our worth in someone else's hands is dangerous. Relying on other people to somehow validate our existence is toxic. It's a losing game. Think about it. How many times have you been told you're too much or perhaps too little? For me, it's happened my entire life. Had I listened to the opinions and external factors around me, I would be lost. I'd be yo-yo-ing back and forth between everyone else's ideals. The target is constantly moving because the target isn't real.

Self-worth comes down to one thing: Knowing who you are and the value you hold. Period. Worthiness can't be found from the outside. It comes from within when we believe in our own abilities and the power within each of us.

Maybe right now, you're struggling to see where you fit within the corporation. You find yourself wondering if anyone sees your value at all or if you're simply just a number. Maybe you've dreamed of doing mission work in Zimbabwe, but you're uncertain how to make an impact. Maybe you recently graduated from college, yet find yourself struggling to land a job and wonder if it was all for nothing. Maybe the loan for your business fell through, or you just got the call from your dream job interview that they selected a more qualified candidate.

Do you believe in your value, and are you willing to fight for it?

Do you believe in the gifts you've been given and the power they hold in creating opportunities when we're met with roadblocks?

Today we stop waiting. We stop doubting and start believing. Are you ready? Rise up.

~~~~~~~~~~~~~~~~~~~~~~~~~~~~~~~~

MOVING FORWARD

We all hinge our self-worth on self-evaluated ideals. Our inner critic is oftentimes our toughest. What ideals are holding you back, both past and present?

Where does the place of unworthiness or not being good enough stem from?

What do you believe you are deserving of in life?

We all have gifts we've been given. Write down your strengths. What are you good at? How can you leverage those in the future?

If you struggle to recognize your gifts, ask a friend to identify what they find valuable in you. Do the characteristics or gifts they describe line up with how you see yourself?

~~~~~~~~~~~~~~~~~~~~~~~~~~~~~~~~

Chapter 24

Behind Closed Doors

Failure Belief: There's only one right way to heal

Before I dive into this story, I want to preface that while it is healthy to lean into community and allow others to be there for you, it's also equally important and sometimes necessary to create boundaries around yourself. To give space to heal in your own time while holding tightly to your journey. Neither is wrong. Not every story needs to be told, but I'm ready now to share mine.

Growing up an only child, I had always wanted to have at least two or three kids. I envisioned a full house and a farm table full of kiddos lined up one by one on the bench. So much so I purchased the table, but it rarely gets used, except for the occasional family get-together or holiday. It turns out my vision would have to stay a dream. We tried for our second a year or so after Grady was born.

I remember being both nervous and excited to see the words "pregnant" on the at-home pregnancy test. I didn't want to have to decipher the lines being faded, one or two, so I stuck with the digital readout for safe measure. I hid the positive pregnancy test in the bathroom drawer and went downstairs to the office. Quickly finding some red cardstock, I cut a heart shape out and wrote the words, "Surprise! You're going to be a daddy, again," in permanent marker, and handed it to my son.

"Go give this to daddy, sweetie."

I watched my husband's face as he read the note. His eyes lit up in surprise.

"Are you serious?" he asked, flashing the biggest smile imaginable.

"Mm-hmm," I said with a grin.

It wasn't long before my baby bump started to pop. It was true. The second does show much faster. I found myself wearing flowy tops and dresses to hide my belly.

For my eight-week appointment, my husband joined me. We were optimistic but also not naïve about what could happen. We had lived that nightmare before, and it had scarred us. Throughout my pregnancy with my son, I held my breath at every appointment, waiting to hear the sweet sounds of his heartbeat until I could officially hold him in my arms.

As we entered the sonographer room, the technician handed me my gown and asked a few questions.

"Is this your first pregnancy?"

"No, it's my second," I said, peeking my head out of the bathroom door. "Well, actually...my third. The first ended in a miscarriage."

I looked over at my husband, who was waiting anxiously in the chair beside the monitor, as I made my way to the examining table.

"Okay," she said. "If you could, go ahead and pull your bottom as far forward as you can, and we'll get started."

I held my breath and stared at the ceiling as I waited for the screen to reveal our little peanut. My eyes widened as I saw what appeared to be two beans inside the gestational sac.

"Is that twins?" I asked, my eyes as wide as saucers.

"Here is baby," she said, pointing to the one on the left. "What you see on the right is an abnormal mass of cells. Nothing looks to have developed there."

"Is that okay?" I asked, fighting back the tears.

"Unfortunately, no. I'm not finding a heartbeat. I'm sorry. The doctor will be in to discuss further." And with that, she walked out.

I stared at my husband in disbelief as tears streamed down my face. I couldn't believe we were here again, but we were. Just then, there was a knock on the door. I wiped the tears from my face and attempted to suck in the snot dripping from my nose.

"Hi, Jenn. I just took a look at the sonogram," my doctor said, giving me a look of sympathy. "I wish I had other news for you. I feel like you've had so many hard things thrown your way. What we see looks to be a partial molar pregnancy. It's incredibly rare and affects about 0.01% of all pregnancies."

"Of course it does," I said sarcastically. "I also had a less than 1% chance my appendix could rupture during birth and we all know how that story goes. So, what do we do?"

"In a partial molar pregnancy, sometimes a fetus will develop, other times it doesn't, but it never survives. In your case, the fetus started to develop but then stopped. That's because partial molar pregnancies typically carry two sets of the father's chromosomes, meaning two sperm fertilized one egg. The other image you were seeing within the gestational sac is a mass of irregular tissues and cells called trophoblasts, also referred to as the mole. The concern becomes when the tissue of the mole is not fully removed. There is a risk of developing a rare cancer known as choriocarcinoma. It's aggressive and something we don't want to mess with. We're going to need to do an immediate D&C, Jenn."

"Okay," I said, fighting back the tears. The word cancer shook me to my core. I had a baby to take care of. He needed me to be here.

"Once the procedure is complete, we'll need to monitor your bloodwork and hCG levels to ensure they are declining. Any elevation would indicate we missed some of the tissue and that it may have attached itself within the uterine wall. At that point, chemotherapy would need to be administered, or an immediate hysterectomy."

My head was spinning with the information being thrown my way. All I could think about was my son and the words cancer and chemotherapy. "How long do we monitor the hCG levels?" my husband asked.

"Six months. For the first month or two we'll be checking every week to ensure we're seeing a sharp enough decline. Then once levels begin to plateau a bit without increasing, we can move to every two weeks, maybe three."

I wanted to scream. The anger and fear that consumed me were overwhelming. While grieving the loss of yet another baby, I was terrified at the thought of not being there for the one I had. I felt selfish for even trying for another one. Never in my wildest dreams did I think wanting to grow my family could cause something like cancer.

My husband and I sat with the scheduler as I waited for them to find the earliest available timeslot for my D&C. I was also referred to a gynecological oncologist to monitor my levels over the next year. After my appointment, my husband and I sat in the car together.

"I'm scared," I confessed in between sobs.

"Me too, but we're going to get through this," he said, kissing my forehead.

"Are you going to go back to work?" I asked.

"Yeah, after I clear my head for a bit. What about you? You're going home, right? You really should rest, baby."

"No, I have a few meetings I really need to attend. Plus, I need to talk to my boss anyway and let her know what's going on."

I drove to work in tears, barely able to see the road in front of me. I was angry. Angry at God and myself. I felt selfish and stupid for even wanting another baby. If I hadn't, I would never be in this position to begin with. As I found a parking spot, I pulled down my car visor to fix my makeup and make myself semi-presentable. I needed to pull myself together. I reached into my purse to apply a bit of lipstick, wiped the underside of my eyes, took a deep breath, and walked inside.

Everyone I passed was utterly oblivious to the pain I held inside. I smiled and asked my co-workers how they were. I listened to their day or their latest family drama while hiding my own. The bathroom quickly became my sanctuary. The cold walls jolted my senses as I leaned against them, hoping for solace from the sadness that consumed me. I felt safe. As if somehow the closeness of the bathroom stall could provide me the privacy and support I needed to grieve. I was far from productive that day, but I needed a place where I couldn't be quiet with my own thoughts for too long. I didn't want to process what had just happened, so I did the only thing I knew; I buried myself in work. I stared at my monitor blankly in between wiping away tears. I tried desperately to focus while in meetings.

People noticed, though. It was blatantly obvious something was wrong, but I refused to acknowledge what it was. I told no one except my boss and my closest friend at work. Each time someone asked how I was, my eyes would well up with tears as I muttered the words, "I'm fine." I lied to their face. On the inside, I was screaming. I wanted to lunge into their arms and tell them, *I'm not fine. I'm anything but okay. I just lost my baby, they used the word cancer at the doctor's office, and I'm terrified!*

But instead, I shut down. I put a wall between myself and everyone else. The thought of saying the words out loud seemed more daunting than if I just kept them locked away inside. I didn't want to deal with other people's emotional responses while processing my own. I didn't need their sympathy or their pity. Saying it out loud made everything real. The thought of hearing someone tell me they're sorry for my loss or that "it's for the best" was enough to send me over the edge. The unwanted pregnancy comments had been enough already. "It's about time for baby number two, don't you think? You don't really want Grady to grow up an only child, do you? Was it hard getting pregnant? Do you guys know how this works? You're not getting any younger, you know." The idea that anyone could understand my pain while uttering undermining comments like that didn't seem feasible. How could they? Even I didn't until I experienced it for myself. Sure, I'd offer up a heartfelt "I'm sorry," but I never truly understood the level of pain they were experiencing. The select few I entrusted with *my* story were those I knew had been there before and who would grieve silently with me.

But why do we choose silence when we are suffering?

Quite simply, we fear emotional exposure. When we are vulnerable, we reveal our truest selves. The deepest, most raw corners of our being, and that can be scary. We worry about what the response may be. So instead, we hide and save our authentic selves for only those we feel safest with. We choose to bleed and cry within the safe harbor and protection of our homes. But by clenching tightly to my truth to protect it from the opinions and reactions of others, I unknowingly denied my own experience. I numbed myself out of fear of being vulnerable. I hid the unworthiness and shame I felt for fear of being truly seen.

I wish I could tell you this was the first time I responded this way, but it's not. It's actually my default mechanism. Whenever something is hard, whenever confrontation presents itself and my emotions are high, I shut down. Instead of processing them, when asked what's wrong, I respond with words like "nothing" or "I'm fine." It can be something as simple as a disagreement with my husband or much larger, like grieving the loss of a loved one, having a miscarriage, losing a job, or waiting on test results. Rather than allowing myself space to feel my emotions, I outwardly deny them. I numb myself. Denial is the body's natural response to allow us space to process our emotions in our own time. Then when we're ready, those feelings and emotions surface and we begin to move through the stages, eventually reaching acceptance and healing.

The next six months turned into nearly twelve. My levels were not declining at the rate the doctors had hoped. They were plateauing. Each weekly test and result was a constant reminder of the life we lost, the life we worried for (my own), and the family we had hoped to build. The mental impact it had on my husband's and my emotional state was profound. The constant worry of cancer or a hysterectomy sat like a rock in the pit of our stomachs. It was as if we were walking around constantly holding our breath, waiting for the other shoe to drop. Around the eleven-month marker, my levels finally flattened. I was in the clear, but we would need to wait a year before trying to conceive again. With two D&Cs, a partial molar pregnancy, along with my age, we decided the risk was too high. We would be a family of three and be thankful.

I held tightly to my story for over five years. It took every bit of that time to work through my own emotions and to process what I went through. The thought of sharing it with others a moment before now seemed terrifying. All of those posts you see on social media of women bravely standing up to say, "I am one in four." I silently read them, whispering, *so am I*. I'm okay saying that out loud now because I've healed silently, on my own terms. I know I'm not broken. The scars I carry tell a story—*my* story. One of heartbreak and loss, trauma, and new beginnings.

It's important to understand there is no wrong way to handle grief or trauma. Some may find support through sharing their experiences and stories, while others may be unwilling to talk about it for a long time. Some of us may grieve in a few short days, while others may take months or even years, like me. I know it's scary to say our truths out loud and to speak and give words to our stories. Vulnerability takes guts, especially when there are no guarantees. We fear our stories may lead to rejection, shame, or loss of relationships, but we are not responsible for how others respond to our pain.

Some people simply won't understand. They won't be able to meet you where you are and process the hurt with you. Others may even make it about themselves, using it as a reason to share their stories, which are always somehow bigger or braver. Others will hastily throw your story to the wind, choosing to divulge your innermost secrets to the world. I get it. The thought of someone adding me to a prayer list or silently judging my inability to easily have children was something I couldn't bear. I needed my story to be mine and mine alone. One I could share when *I* felt ready.

That time is now. In choosing to share my story, I do so by writing it for the world to read in my words, not someone else's interpretation of my journey. The stigma that comes with pregnancy loss, or a woman's ability to conceive at all, is one that needs to be removed. The backhanded comments, the side eyes, and the judgments must stop. You don't know her story, and quite frankly, you don't need to. Sometimes our business is simply to mind our own. To pay attention to what we project and the impact our words and responses have on others.

Last spring, the three of us were walking through the gated community down the road. My son feverishly peddled his bike while we walked alongside him. A younger couple was outside re-doing the landscaping around their house while their little girl played outside.

"He's getting pretty big," the man yelled. "About time for an-other one, don't you think?"

"We're happy with one, thanks!" We waved with a smile.

He looked at his wife, confused, and shrugged his shoulders.

"If only he knew our story," I told my husband, shaking my head.

A woman's wholeness does not come from our womb and what we can or can't produce. Some of the bravest, most impactful wom-en I know have never birthed a child of their own, yet they mentor, foster, adopt, or advocate for children every single day.

I know what it's like to be on the reciprocating end, to be going through something so deeply personal and internal you fear sharing it with anyone. If I could offer you one bit of advice, it would be this:

Whatever you are going through, you are not broken. You are not any less whole because of your choices or your circumstances. Others' inability to meet you where you are is simply a reflection of their own journey. It is not yours to hold. You can't effectively fight your own battles while gripping everyone else's responses tightly in your hands.

It's okay to protect your peace and allow yourself the space to heal on your own terms. It doesn't make you wrong or any less brave. Sure, I know there is power in being vulnerable. It's why I chose to share this story when I did, but I also recognize the strength it takes to honor yourself and the time you need.

You aren't required to be an open book unless you want to be. You get to decide what you write. You can choose to tell twenty-five people or no one at all. The choice is yours. The boundary is yours to set. People don't have to know your story, but they do need to respect your journey.

~~~~~~

MOVING FORWARD

What things from the past have shaped how you respond to vulnerability and the need to hold it all in?

Identify what it is you're afraid of that may be keeping you from being vulnerable (i.e.: rejection, shame, need for belonging, sense of unworthiness)

Remember acknowledging and accepting our own emotional feelings is the first step to being vulnerable; then we must work to share those feelings with others.

~~~~~~

Chapter 25

Ch-Ch-Ch - Changes

Failure Belief: Too much change is a bad thing

I hate change. Scratch that; I loathe it. Regardless of how big or small something may seem, the thought of change sends me into a tailspin of anxiety. Want me to move desks? Why must you torture me? I like it here. Want to talk about changing jobs or career paths? I might actually throw up. Kid starting kindergarten? No, I have not had five years to prep for this! It's too much, too soon. I am not ready. I like consistency and routine. I like to know what I can expect and when to expect it. I have an acrylic calendar where I keep track of our sporting events, school activities, and appointments. All of which are color-coordinated. I also have a planner, where I house this information on paper. Why I need to duplicate my efforts I have zero clue. Something about wiping it off each month gives me anxiety.

My husband makes fun of me all the time. I'm a serial planner. I can't wing it if I tried. I ask the boys all the time, "What do you want to do this weekend? Go to the park, zoo, play some baseball?" You name it; the sky's the limit. I just need to know what that limit is *today*. You know, before we get to tomorrow, so I can plan. I realize this is ridiculous, but we're all a work in progress. Truthfully, I am secretly envious of my husband's ability to be Mr. Fun Squad. The man will literally wake up on a random Saturday and decide it's *daddy day*. What this means, I don't really know because they NEVER HAVE A PLAN! Believe me, I ask, and I'm typically met with something like, "We don't know. We haven't decided yet." Huh...sounds adventurous. Fun with a capital F. Except it is. My son loves these types of days. For him, it's like a build-your-own sundae. It's adventure in a Ram truck with dad, who can wing it like the best of them.

For me, change is a dirty word. One I try my best to avoid, even the kind that can lead to adventures. Something about the unknown riddles me with anxiety, even if it's unknown fun. But in 2020, a change was lurking that none of us could prepare for. On March 15, the entire world went into lockdown. Schools closed, child care services shuttered their windows, and businesses went remote as our lives were flipped upside down. Working mothers and parents everywhere quickly found themselves juggling the role of caregiver, teacher, and employee as our worlds collided. There was seemingly no way out. Choose to juggle it all or quit your job. The choice is yours.

It was the biggest change many of us had ever endured.

Little voices and squishy faces adorned our zoom calls as we attempted to teach math lessons while simultaneously hosting the latest budget meeting. It was hard, both emotionally and physically. A lot of grace was needed during that time as we all navigated uncharted waters. But as we made our way to the other side, I realized something. Change, while scary, is doable. I had confronted the biggest change our world has encountered in a long time, and I was still standing. Maybe change wasn't as bad as I made it out to be.

Stay with me here. I promise I haven't lost my mind. My point is if we can face a global pandemic, we can surely change jobs or move to a new city. We can enroll in college or write a book. We can face our diagnosis head-on or tackle our finances. We can look the big, bad, scary change in the face and say, up yours.

In full honesty, I had complained about my lack of career progression for years. I wanted things to change but kept waiting for

someone else to create it for me. I allowed others to define my career path instead of taking charge of my own. Have you ever picked
up a carton of eggs, only to bring it home and find one busted,
leaving a big pile of messy goo everywhere? I have. For me, the
busted egg was change. I allowed my fear to leak out in every facet
of my life. Rather than throw the one bad egg out and clean up the
others, I was willing to throw the whole carton away. I was content
staying where I was to avoid the mess.

Right now, you're probably wondering, so what did you do? I
did what any middle-aged woman would do. With my career at a
standstill and my one and only baby heading off to kindergarten, I
decided to shake things up.

I spoke up more. I voiced what I wanted out of my career and
what I was no longer willing to accept. I even decided to write a
book because why couldn't I? I met life in the moment, right where
I was. I was no longer afraid of change. I stopped running from it
and instead sought it out.

And in doing so, I felt empowered.

Now did my world change in an instant? No, but I did land a
book deal and a pay raise. I learned something else, too. I learned
that I couldn't expect change if I'm unwilling to change myself.

That one was painful, but a necessary ah-ha moment, none-
theless.

We all make choices every single day. We choose our partners,
our homes, our careers, and our friendships. But what we've failed
to learn is that we're human, and with being human comes growth.
Change becomes inevitable, yet we cling to what we know even if
it no longer serves us. Our human nature is to deny change. We
become set in our ways and creatures of habit. We hold tight to
complacency and consistency, touting it's our choice, but is it? Or
is it our fear holding us hostage? Maybe it's an opportunity for a
new job or a new home. Maybe it's to study abroad or an acceptance letter into grad school: do you deny it or embrace it?

Human nature points us to automatic rejection. By default, we
begin thinking of all the reasons we shouldn't move forward with

whatever change it may be. Fear of the unknown paralyzes us, so we accept our complacency as a way of life. We numb ourselves to this constant state of surviving instead of thriving. Even while subconsciously knowing that this "thing" may no longer be serving us. Knowing that maybe this friendship, relationship, or job isn't what is best for me. It's creating toxicity and negativity in my life, but still, we stay. Our fear takes hold telling us we're fine when we're anything but the word.

Surviving is just what we do.

We would rather stay comfortably miserable than step into something unknowingly meaningful, yet risky. Change instigates our fight-or-flight response. We go into survival mode and begin to anticipate impending doom as our brain senses potential danger. This is good for survival but not always for navigating basic life. The problem with change is it disrupts our routine.

However, life cannot be lived without experiencing some amount of change. So how do we cope and better equip ourselves to accept change, and sometimes even seek it out? Dr. Carla Shuman identified in *Psychology Today* a few key ways to help us navigate change (commentary is mine).

1. "Acknowledge both negative and positive emotions around the change" – We all know change can happen when we least expect it. Working in corporate America, I can't tell you how many organizational changes, layoffs, and job moves I've dealt with. Each left me with a flood of emotions as I processed my lack of control over the situation. However, if I didn't allow myself room to feel those emotions, I would never reach a place of acceptance. I would be stuck in defense mode and resist the change even more.

2. "Make a list of what has changed and what will be different" – Knowing and understanding my role within the change allows me to better accept and prepare for the unknown. Even when we anticipate the change that happens, it doesn't necessarily mean we are prepared for all of the

implications that come along with it. By writing them down, we are less surprised and feel more equipped to handle our emotions.

3. "Seek emotional support from people you trust" – This one is huge. Make no mistake, we are not talking about needing advice or someone to point out that we should see the good in losing our job. This is centered around emotional support and understanding. When navigating a change, we want to be seen and heard. It's imperative to surround yourself with those who will meet you with empathy and provide you the necessary support.

Plain and simple, we run in the opposite direction of change because we don't know the outcome. But the question we fail to ask ourselves is, "What's the risk if we don't?" I'll tell you, for thirty-plus years, I let our culture dictate what I should aspire to and what dreams I should have as a woman. For years, it was head down, do the work, and be grateful without ever asking the simple question *why*? Or even better, *does this serve me*? Does this align with where I see my life and what I want for my future? I was afraid to change because I had adopted someone else's ideals. My complacency won over.

The risk of not taking a chance meant I stalled out. I had climbed as far as I would go without stepping into the unknown.

Maybe you're there too. Maybe you've denied change for fear of the unknown, but a life lived in fear isn't one I'm willing to accept anymore, and I hope you'll do the same. You don't have to stay married to the status quo. There's a whole life out there waiting to be lived. So, take a chance, risk it, and go get it.

MOVING FORWARD

What fears are holding you back from making a change in your life?

What are some positive thoughts about yourself that you can focus on to counteract those fears?

What is the opportunity that could arise from creating or facing change?

If we are honoring our values and pushing beyond contentment, what changes would you need to make in order to live in complete alignment?

Chapter 26

Glass Ceilings

Failure Belief: Women shouldn't be ambitious

How many times have you come across an outspoken woman? Perhaps you were sitting in a meeting or attempting to collaborate on a school project. Maybe you signed up to help with the school party or volunteered for a charitable event, but whatever it was, I guarantee we've all come across *her*. You know the one I'm talking about. You can already picture her in your mind, can't you? She talks too much, has a million and one questions, and an opinion about everything. She's clearly *bossy* or a *bitch*, right? Women don't speak up like that. Anyone that does must be completely full of herself. Why doesn't she sit quietly like the rest of us?

Listen, I've been guilty of labeling women the infamous B word, but I've also been on the receiving end of that label. I grew up moderately confident. I guess I never got the memo that I needed to dial it down. I just did me, and that bothered people...a lot of people. I should also add that I was quiet (I know it's hard to believe), which didn't help my case at all. Quiet plus confident is never a good combo. You quickly become labeled stuck up. I remember the first time someone called me a bitch. It was my sophomore year of high school. I couldn't even tell you why it happened. I just remember it stung. It turns out it would be the first of many. At the age of forty, I can tell you I've heard it all. I've been called bossy, a bitch, slut, whore, cunt, and every other name you can think of simply for existing.

It's hard not to internalize those words and sink down. The idea of being thrown yet another label makes the sidelines look more appealing. Our ambition takes the back seat as our passion dwindles, but I guarantee you it didn't always feel this way.

Girls don't start out timid and soft-spoken. It's something that is learned. There are plenty of ambitious, confident girls out there who aren't afraid of speaking up. Their voices are boisterous with a fearlessness that is unmatched. They know exactly who they are and they're not afraid to share it with the world until the world turns on them and informs them they're too much. So, they shrink down. They internalize people's disappointments and begin believing they should change. They begin letting the boys raise their hands even when they know the answer, but make no mistake; that little girl is still in there, full of fire and fury.

Girlfriends, we live in the twenty-first century. If having opinions, ignoring unwanted advances, asking valid questions, fighting for equality, and speaking up for what I believe in bothers someone, hold my coffee because we're about to heat things up. Knowing who you are and what you want out of life isn't wrong. It doesn't make you a *bitch*. It makes people uncomfortable, which makes *you* a threat. Let's face it; our entire culture and patriarchal system was built on the unilateral power of men. It's not the fault of any one individual in particular. It's just what it was. However, as women progress and acquire more seats at the table, things are shifting. But the stigma that comes with a woman's ambition is still a dicey one. Ambition in men is rewarded. In us, it becomes our penalty. When women speak up, we challenge the status quo. Society does its best to keep us in check by labeling and placing us into boxes.

In her book, *A Radical Awakening*, Dr. Shefali writes:

The more we honor our voices and claim our power, the more we are going to be called a bitch. Culture doesn't like empowered women who speak up for themselves. Calling us bitches is one of the ways culture controls its powerful women. When we understand this, we stop taking these words personally. We understand that pissing people off comes with the territory. When people are pissed off, they seek to silence the other using shaming terms. After all, how dare we change the rules of the game.

Take a look at any corporation today, and you can quickly see the threshold to which women and marginalized minorities are held to. You could practically draw a line on the career progression chart where it all stops. Women continue to be significantly underrepresented at a leadership level across all organizations. Ann Friedman, writer for *Elle* magazine, writes, "No matter how hard we hustle, the statistics say that most of us will still hit that proverbial glass ceiling—especially if we are women of color and/or parents, and most especially if we are parents of more than one child." As women, when we speak, we tether between being too aggressive or completely ignored. We're either too much or too little. We simply can't win.

She's right. For years, I took the bait. I defined my ambition through the pursuit of salaries and titles. I bought into the idea that if I hustled enough I could make it; yet nothing changed no matter how hard I worked. When I entered motherhood, I quickly found myself burned out and overwhelmed. I had a choice. I could continue to try to reach for new heights, aspiring to find my place in a male-dominated workforce, or I could pick and choose what served me. I could create and redefine what ambition meant for me.

Do I still want to shatter glass ceilings? Absolutely, but in a healthier, more positive way that empowers women to have a choice in what ambition looks like for each one of us. One that emboldens us to take a firm grip on our lives and the choices that align with what we hope to obtain—and I'm not alone. Women everywhere are no longer satisfied simply climbing the corporate ladder; it's not just about the job or the title anymore. Instead, we're in search of corporations that harbor inclusion. Businesses that place emphasis on things like equality, flexible working environments, affordable healthcare options, and an office culture that prioritizes mental wellness.

It's not that women don't want to work; we simply want to work for businesses that work for us. We're tired of singlehandedly trying to foster an environment that works for all and not reaping the reward ourselves. According to the McKinsey *Women in the Workplace 2022 study,* three key reasons were identified when talking about why women leaders were leaving their companies, one of which was work culture. "If companies don't take action in response to these trends, they're at risk of losing more women leaders. That could have serious implications. Compared to men at the same level, women leaders are investing more time and energy in effective people management, allyship, and DEI. They are leading the transition to a more supportive, inclusive workplace, which is what the next generation of employees—and especially younger women—want and expect."

Our ambition is not lost; we've chosen to redefine it in a way that works for the modern woman and the next generation. Our hands are tired from banging on the glass ceiling for decades, only to make a few cracks. They can have the ceiling. It's time to blow off the whole roof and tip it on its side. Ambition and tenacity aren't dirty words. A woman or minority should never be penalized for having them. It's not about luck or being in the right place at the right time. You can be grateful for what you have, be proud of what you've done, and still want more. You can love where you are and what you've accomplished but demand healthier boundaries. You can ambitiously pursue whatever you want. It's time to take it back. Our way. A female revolution of bold choices, ones we own and go after with a fierceness that can't be denied.

Maybe for you, you're ambitiously pursuing a life of balance. A life of health and purpose. One that allows you time to care for your children or elderly parents. Maybe you're seeking to be bold in your asks and what you need. Maybe there's a dream you'd love to pursue. A new project or hobby that's been burning deep within your belly. Look at me; I achieved one of my biggest goals at forty. After over a year and a half of countless rejections, and a whole lot of persistence, this book found its home. Ambition looks different for everyone, but society will no longer label us for having it.

We won't be branded as *bitchy* or *bossy*. The universal traits that have existed for so long that assign us to what box we should or shouldn't be in are being disassembled. It no longer matters your age, race, or what gene pool you are or aren't a part of. Whether it's starting your own business, being a stay-at-home mom of four, flying solo, or sitting as vice president of a multi-million-dollar corporation, you get to decide. Ambition is yours to define. Never let anyone make you feel smaller for having it. It's yours to own with reckless abandonment.

MOVING FORWARD

Ambition means something different to each of us. Define what ambition means to you.

How do you define success?

How can we encourage our daughters to use their voices and advocate for themselves?

How can we educate the men and boys in our life to champion women and girls to use their voices?

HEALING & HOLDING
OUR TRUTHS

Chapter 27

Reclaiming My Joy

Our local homeless shelter sits about a block from my office, its neon cross serving as a beacon of hope for many. I vividly remember growing up craning my neck as we crested over the bridge, trying to catch a glimpse of its light. I wondered what it was like inside that building, what the men thought, and how they looked. And in that moment, while fogging up the glass of my window, I made a silent commitment to myself to always look for the good.

When I first got relocated for work to right downtown, I could feel the pull. It seemed only natural that I help, but how? My contribution started out small, walking across the street over my lunch break to serve meals to the men every Wednesday. For forty-five minutes, it wasn't about me. It wasn't about the day I had or even the day I hadn't had; it was about serving others. I began to know these men, not just at face value, but their names and their stories. I learned how one man lost his job, and another was battling end-stage Parkinson's, a disease which his family didn't have the means to deal with, and so they dropped him off at the shelter. I learned of their addictions and their struggles. I began recognizing them on the streets, at the nearest park bench, or on their morning walks around the block. I saw them not as just someone loitering around town but as people...real people with families and children.

After a few months, two of my co-workers and friends asked to join me. I happily accepted the company, and we became known amongst the men as *Charlie's Angels*. The three of us, adorned with our smiles, would make small talk with the men as they went through the line, always polite and grateful. We would ask about their day and how they were. Most would utter something vague like, "Fine, thank you," while flashing a grin. My friends and I would talk amongst ourselves during that time, mostly about work or the latest with our families, but I'll never forget one particular day.

The day had been a disaster. A rushed daycare drop-off and kiss goodbye meant another botched morning in the books. Nothing had gone right, and it was only 8:38 a.m. Late for work per usual, I fumbled to open my laptop while sitting at a red light, desperate to locate the dial-in information for the meeting that was already underway. As I threw my hands up in the air, I prayed the woman in front of me would reach within herself and find the same sense of urgency I had in that moment and just drive or change lanes altogether, but unfortunately, today was not that day. I could feel my face turning red as my heart raced. *Why does every morning have to be like this?* I thought. Disorganized, discombobulated, and distracted, that's how I started most days. Despite my best efforts to locate my umbrella, I had left it where I always do—on the kitchen counter with my lunch, of course. It looked like my laptop bag would have to suffice. As I ran into the office with my bag held over my head, every inch of me got soaked. It didn't help that I had failed to even check the weather before leaving the house and had chosen to wear the most sensible shoe imaginable...flip-flops. Yeah, it was that kind of morning.

I had only been up and going for three hours, but it felt more like three days.

As I entered the revolving doors, I remembered it was Wednesday, which meant one thing; mission day. But honestly, I wasn't feeling it at all.

Do you ever have those times where you commit to something, but once the day arrives, you're not interested? Like not in the slightest. All you can think about is canceling, wondering why in the world you ever thought the idea sounded good in the first place. That was me, especially after the morning I had just had.

But if there is one thing I hate more than doing something I don't want to do, it's disappointing someone. So, I went. As I made my way down to the basement where the kitchen was, I smelled the sweet aroma of homemade apple pie and all the comfort foods. I could feel my mood beginning to shift. Today had sucked, but I was here trying to find the good. I was greeting the men as they entered the line when a tall gentleman I didn't recognize approached the window. He flashed his big toothy grin at me. "Well, hi there. How are you?" I said, smiling back.

"I'm blessed, and you?"

Enter the gut check.

This man had nothing to his name except the clothes on his back and a backpack he stowed away at the front desk, yet he had enough joy and perspective to realize he was alive. He had a warm meal and a place to lay his head. He was thankful. You want to talk about shifting my perspective. Ten minutes earlier, I was just complaining about the annoying weather, how the day had gotten away from me, and how I was behind on life...and he feels blessed.

And in that moment, it hit me. Somewhere along the way, joy had become this illusion, a bargaining chip that can only be manufactured through stores or the latest trends. Every single day we are bombarded with ad after ad telling us how to find our joy. Buy this anti-aging cream so you can look and feel younger. Drive this car, and you'll be sure to turn heads. Purchase this diet plan to get the body of your dreams. So we do what any normal person would do; we chase it and cling to it with everything we have. We accumulate things and buy into the latest trends. We finance cars and purchase our dream homes, only to be left empty.

But joy isn't a trophy you can hang on a wall or a fancy car parked in your garage. You're not going to find it in designer clothes, the latest fad diets, or the title you carry—it's how you *live*. We have to stop objectifying and idolizing the very things that are stealing our joy.

That joy you're searching so hard for? You're simply looking in all the wrong places. It's not found in things; it's right in front of you.

It's the mess you've cleaned for the fiftieth time and the kids laughing in the living room. Okay, maybe not the mess. I know that drives you crazy, but I promise those tiny humans will make it in the real world without you one day. It's building a life together, no matter how messy and chaotic. It's fighting for your marriage through the not-so-great times only to emerge on the other side stronger than ever. It's getting up with tired, bloodshot eyes knowing that today you get one more day on this earth. You get to breathe fresh air and feel the warmth of the sun on your face. It's your health and the food you put on the table, regardless of the fact that it's chicken nuggets and Kraft Mac n' Cheese for the fourth day in a row.

And yet every single day, we're missing it.

I'm not saying that vacuuming or scrubbing toilets will ever really bring me any sense of joy, but the little people that make the messes do, and that matters. Sometimes I think we get so caught up in everything we believe our life isn't that we forget to see all the blessings staring us right in the face.

Thankfully, on a rainy day in July, one man shifted my perspective and handed me a big slice of humble pie without even knowing it. Life is funny like that. One minute you think you're helping others, only to find, in reality, they're helping you.

He was waiting for my answer to his simple—and yet not simple at all—question. How was I?

"I'm blessed," I said with a smile. And you know what? For the first time in a long time, I actually believed it. Not for how the day had gone but for the simple fact that I was there to experience it. I was breathing and alive. I felt joyful.

You see, joy is not a destination you'll arrive at, and you never struggle to find happiness another day in your life. It's a state of being. A choice and conscious effort to practice gratitude every single day. Is it easy? No. Some days it's next to impossible, but if a man at a shelter has enough perspective to recognize his blessings, then I have to believe we can too. Look for the joy, and when you find it, make sure to choose it every single day.

~~~~~~~~~~~~~~~~~~~~~~~~~~~~~~~~~~~~~~

MOVING FORWARD

As women, our lives are hectic and oftentimes a blur, but we all have the ability to harness joy. List out the things that bring you happiness.

What tangible ways can you work to feel connected to the joy those things bring?

~~~~~~~~~~~~~~~~~~~~~~~~~~~~~~~~~~~~~~

Chapter 28

Pebbles & Sand

You may have heard a story called, "The Jar of Life." While its origins are unknown, it gained popularity when Stephen Covey wrote about it in his book, *First Things First*. It's been told countless ways, but today, I want to use a beautiful illustration created by Meir Kay between a professor and his students.

In this video, a philosophy professor enters the room, placing an empty mason jar on the desk. Then, grabbing a box of golf balls, he begins filling the jar.

"Is the jar full?" He asks the class, to which they agree it is.

He then reaches into his briefcase to reveal a cup full of pebbles and begins adding them to the golf ball filled jar. "What about now?" he asks. "Is the jar full?"

"Yes," the students reply, smiling at one another.

Producing a cup of sand, the professor pours it into the jar. The sand fills all the gaps left by the golf balls and pebbles.

"And how about now? Is the jar full now?" He asks. "Yes," the students respond.

The professor then grabs a cup of coffee from within his briefcase and empties it into the mason jar.

He goes on to explain that the jar illustrates our life. The golf balls represent everything that is important to you. Your family, relationships, passions, health, connection, all the things that give meaning and purpose to our lives. The pebbles are the other things that matter, like our jobs, car, homes, finances, etc. The sand is everything else. The noise. The minuscule things that fill up our day-to-day. The sand is our failure beliefs. The things we obsess over as we try desperately to fit this mold of perfection.

When we put the sand in first, what happens? There's no room for the golf balls or the pebbles, right? The same can be said for our lives. When we focus our time and energy on the sand, the failure beliefs we now know to be a lie, we leave no space for the things that matter.

You now have the tools necessary to stake claim over your jar. Be intentional about setting your priorities in your life. Are you simply filling your life jar with sand, or are you focusing on what's most important to you first? There will always be time to do laundry or tackle the dishes.

We have the power to protect our own happiness and peace by prioritizing our life one golf ball at a time.

Before class adjourned, one of the students raised their hand and asked what the cup of coffee represented. The professor smiled, "I'm glad you asked. It goes to show you that no matter how full your life may seem, you always have time for a coffee and a chat with a friend."

He's right. This idea that we don't have enough time is wrong. The coffee doesn't spill over. It's absorbed by the sand, filling all of the cracks. Such a beautiful and powerful illustration of how we can shift our priorities, expectations, and mindset to the things that truly matter to us.

What are you giving weight to today? Are you focusing your time and intention on things that don't matter? Or are you giving weight to things that you value and cherish? Your life is yours. Write down the things that are most important to you, and focus on those first. The rest will fill in the gaps to create a life of joy and purpose.

~~~~~~~~~~~~~~~~~~~~~~~~~~~~~~~~

MOVING FORWARD

What are the golf balls in your life? List them out and be intentional about placing them first.

~~~~~~~~~~~~~~~~~~~~~~~~~~~~~~~~

Chapter 29

Free

As we close, you may find yourself feeling overwhelmed. We've deconstructed so many failure beliefs and lies we've held onto. We've flipped our world upside down, the one we knew to be right and just, and placed it on its head. This can trigger feelings of anger, disappointment, denial, and even pain. Just know that everything you're experiencing is normal. The failure beliefs we've uncovered have taken me years to dissect and overcome. Nothing happened overnight, but we now understand it was all just sand.

I recently listened to an episode of the *We Can Do Hard Things* podcast with Glennon Doyle that focused on this very thing. The journey of healing. Her guest for this particular episode was author and activist, Alex Elle. Alex said something that resonated with me when she said, "Healing is our love offering to the world. When we heal *our* world, we begin to heal *the* world. When we see *ourselves*, we start to see *other people*."

What a beautiful offering. To be seen and to see others. We control our priorities and our jar, and while it's not been an easy journey, I can tell you what you'll find on the other side—an abundant life filled with hope, love, acceptance, joy, and peace.

All you have to do is honor one truth—your own. *This* is your guiding compass, not the world or any other external variables, just—you. Every flaw, quirk, belief, and dream that makes you who you are is worthy of being seen. You no longer need to hide your truest self. I hope you believe it. I hope you go boldly into the night, unafraid to claim your authentic divinity. I hope you know exactly who you are, what you care about, and the triggers that sit within you that cause you to doubt. I hope you name them one by one, calling them out for the lies they are. I hope you refuse to sit quietly on the sidelines of your life and instead choose to harness it with a fierceness that people can't help but notice. I hope you share your gifts with the world. The weird ones, the ones that make an impact, the talents that spark joy in yourself and others; all of them. I hope you see what a gift they are and what a gift *you* are. I hope you break every box and mold you've ever been placed in and refuse to use them to cage in others. I hope you face every barrier and road-block meant to deter you head-on with fearlessness. I hope you no longer search for the approval of others but find it within yourself. I hope you claim your space and take it up unapologetically. I hope you drop comparison and instead choose to root for the woman beside you, grabbing her hand and pulling her up alongside you. I hope you lose the weight of unwanted expectations, so you can see that everything you're searching for already exists within you. Embrace it. Protect it. Fight for it, and live unapologetically—you.

Forever in your corner,
Jenn

MOVING FORWARD

What do you not want to believe in anymore?

What are some things that you will work on believing every day about yourself that you know to be true?

What are those things you can practice and remind yourself of?

Acknowledgments

There have been many individuals who inspired, encouraged, and empowered me to write these pages. To my Creator, the one whose whispers were the loudest. Your relentless pursuit of me and this message have been undeniable. While these words and stories are mine, I know you were the author. I can see your fingerprints on all of it. Thank you for opening my eyes and setting me free. I pray these words shake women everywhere to their core, reminding them of who they were designed to be.

To my husband, Jim. My best friend, biggest cheerleader, and love of my life. You took a long time, but you were worth the wait. Thank you for entrusting me to share our story; one of heartbreak and healing along with abundant joy. You've seen me at my worst. You've held the broken pieces of my heart and helped me piece them back together. But make no mistake; I wouldn't change it for the world. This life we've built together is one I'm thankful for each and every day. You saw something bellowing deep within me and forced it to the surface. You accept every bit of my stubbornness and challenge me in ways I never thought possible. You drive me crazy and make me laugh like no other. You are my rock, my safe place, and my home. Thank you for safeguarding my dreams and encouraging me to dream bigger. Your faith in me is unwavering.

To the one who made me a mama, bug, you are my world. Before I held you in my arms, I loved you. Watching you grow has been the joy of my life. Thank you for making me a mother. The woman I am today is because of you. Never let the world dim your light. Stand firm in your convictions. Love with your whole heart and seek Jesus in all you do. Work to see the best in people. Fight to be others' voices. Judge no one. Respect others. Love BIG and always be kind. Thank you for broadening my world and restoring my faith. I can't wait to see who you become. My greatest accomplishment and privilege is and always will be raising you and watching you soar. I love you.

They say you are who you surround yourself with. Lucky for me, I have a proven track record of strong, fierce women in my life, preferably served up with a side of wit and sass for good measure and humor. To know them is to love them. They are my people.

First, to Kels. The universe knew our paths needed to cross three years ago, and I am grateful every day that they did. Your friendship is such a gift. Thank you for being willing to go deep in conversation with me and for our countless voice memos and rants back and forth. The journey of finding ourselves is not easy, but it's easier with friends like you. Keep shining your light and chasing life with reckless abandonment. You are such a gift to this world and an amazing human. Knowing you is an honor.

To my sis. Kendra, where would I be without you? Five years ago, two writers who had never met became the best of friends. One in Illinois and the other in Kentucky. I thank God for you each and every day. Your ability to talk me off a ledge or gently call me out when I need it is one I rely on. So much of this book has our conversations seeped within the pages. Every lesson learned. Every victory and defeat. We have seen one another through it all; the lowest of lows and highest of highs. I don't think you realize how special you are, so I'm writing it where you'll never forget it. You inspire me, deepen my faith, and encourage me to be better every single day.

To my lifeline friend, Jen. Who knew back in 2004 our friendship would span over two decades? You inspired me then, and you continue to today. You embody what it means to be a strong leader, advocate, role model, and fierce woman. Thank you for being my biggest cheerleader. Your heart for others is relentless. Here's to countless more years of laughing til we can't breathe over chips and queso, trips to Italy, and memories for a lifetime. You have me in your corner forever. I love you.

To my bestie, Rachel, all those years sitting silently in nearby church pews, never saying a word because we were too shy. I guess God knew we needed one another. From college to our wedding day, we've stood by one another. We've vacationed together, cried, laughed, and stayed up way too late. You hold secrets no one else knows, and I keep yours. From Rhonda Vincent concerts, orange energy drinks, and blow torches, I owe all my fun times to you.

Home is not a place. It's a feeling. To my mom and dad, I know it wasn't always easy growing up, but I never knew. The amount of hard work and dedication you put into building a home filled with love is one I will cherish forever. It's true, you never fully understand the sacrifice your parents made until you become one yourself. From chauffeuring me to sports to coaching, teaching, guiding, and cheering, you were there for all of it. The one constant in my life was you. While Dad gets recognition for my stubbornness and determination, I owe my heart to you, Mom. I love you both.

To my girls in Wyoming, thank you for restoring my faith and trusting me to hold your stories. In doing so, you gave me the strength to share mine. Each of you holds a special place in my heart. I love you BIG!

To preacher, aka, David. How different the world would be if we all loved like you do. Your ability to meet people where they are is a gift. Never change. There are so many people out there desperately wanting to simply be seen and loved, both of which you do so well. Thank you for your openness to go against the grain and challenge the status quo, not out of defiance but out of love. Keep being light. I love you, friend!

To my literary agent, Tina Wainscott, thank you for taking a chance on my book. Your ability to see the larger picture while gently challenging me to dig deeper made this book what it is today. Thank you for believing in me and guiding me through this entire process.

To *Urano World*, my editor, Lydia, and everyone else who helped bring this book to life. Thank you for embracing my vision and inviting me to share my story with the world. I am forever grateful.

Finally, to my readers, thank you will never be enough. Whether you are new to this space or have been with me since the beginning, I love you. So often, people tell me how my words inspired them, but the reality is you inspire me every day. The stories you share with me are ones filled with triumph and heartbreak, and I am here for all of it. Rooting for you, fiercely defending you, celebrating with you, and holding you close. You are not alone.

Notes & Resources

Chapter 1

Brown, Brené. *Daring Greatly*. Avery, 2012, p. 131,
　　https://brenebrown.com/book/daring-greatly/

Chapter 3

Tatakovsky, Margarita. "The Power in Being Still and How to
　　Practice Stillness." *Psych Central*, 5 July 2022,
　　https://psychcentral.com/blog/
　　the-power-in-being-still-how-to-practice-stillness.

Chapter 5

Clear, James. "How Willpower Works: How to Avoid Bad
　　Decisions." Jamesclear.com. https://jamesclear.com/
　　willpower-decision-fatigue.

Robbins, Mel. "5 Essential Hacks I'm Using to Make New Habits
　　Stick (No. 32)." *The Mel Robbins Podcast*, 15 Jan. 2023,
　　https://podcasts.apple.com/us/podcast/5-essential-hacks-im-
　　using-to-make-new-habits-stick/
　　id1646101002?i=1000594561411.

Keller, Jan, et al. "Habit formation following routine-based versus
　　time-based cue planning: A randomized controlled trial."

British Journal of Health Psychology, vol. 26, no. 3, 2021, pp. 807-824, dx.doi.org/10.1111/bjhp.12504.

Maxwell, John C. The 15 *Invaluable Laws of Growth: Live Them and Reach Your Potential*. Center Street, 2014.

Chapter 7

Castrillon, Caroline. "How Women Can Stop Apologizing and Take Their Power Back." *Forbes*, 14 July 2019, https://www.forbes.com/sites/carolinecastrillon/2019/07/14/how-women-can-stop-apologizing-and-take-their-power-back/?sh=699248084ce6.

Chapter 8

Brown, Brené. "Brené with Emily and Amelia Nagoski on Burnout and How to Complete the Stress Cycle." *Unlocking Us with Brené Brown*, 14 October 2020, https://brenebrown.com/podcast/brene-with-emily-and-amelia-nagoski-on-burnout-and-how-to-complete-the-stress-cycle/.

Chapter 11

Edlynn, Emily. "Yelled at Your Kids? Here's Why You Should Let Go of That Shame." *The Washington Post*, 13 May 2021, https://www.washingtonpost.com/lifestyle/2021/05/13/yelling-parents-children-discipline-guilt/.

Chapter 12

Bustle Contributor. "How to Get Better at Saying No." *Huffington Post*, 6 December 2017, https://www.huffpost.com/entry/how-to-say-no_b_10737678.

Chapter 13

Sanok, Joe. "A Guide to Setting Better Boundaries."
    Harvard Business Review, 14 April 2022,
    https://hbr.org/2022/04/a-guide-to-setting-better-boundaries.

Chapter 16

Resource: https://news.un.org/en/story/2022/06/1120682
    https://singlemotherguide.com/single-mother-statistics/.

Chapter 17

Doyle, Glennon, et al. "Sonya Renee Taylor: What if
    You Loved Your Body (No. 168)." *We Can Do
    Hard Things with Glennon Doyle*, 9 November 2022,
    https://podcasts.apple.com/us/podcast/sonya-renee-taylor-
    what-if-you-loved-your-body/
    id1564530722?i=1000593882497.

Hatmaker, Jen. *Fierce, Free, and Full of Fire: The Guide to Being
    Glorious You.* Nelson Books, 2020, pp. 44-45.

Chapter 18

Haas, Susan. "How to Stop Comparing Yourself
    to Others." *Psychology Today*, 15 March 2018,
    https://www.psychologytoday.com/us/blog/prescriptions-
    life/201803/how-stop-comparing-yourself-others.

Shetty, Jay. "7 Ways to Stop Comparing Yourself to Others."
    Jay Shetty Podcast, https://jayshetty.me/
    podcast/7-ways-to-stop-comparing-yourself-to-others/.

Chapter 20

Davis, Tchiki. "Five Steps to Finding Your Life Purpose." *Psychology Today*, 12 Dec. 2017, https://www.psychologytoday.com/us/blog/click-here-happiness/201712/five-steps-finding-your-life-purpose.

Dr. Shefali. *A Radical Awakening*. Harper Collins, 2021, p. 303.

Chapter 21

Robbins, Mel. "Why Is Adult Friendship So Hard? 5 Lies You Tell Yourself & the Truth You Need to Hear (No. 9)." *The Mel Robbins Podcast*, 30 October 2022, https://podcasts.apple.com/us/podcast/why-is-adult-friendship-so-hard-5-lies-you-tell-yourself/id1646101002?i=1000584444019.

Chapter 22

Clark, Nancy. "Act Now to Shrink the Confidence Gap." *Forbes*. April 28, 2014. https://www.forbes.com/sites/carolinecastrillon/2022/10/16/how-to-cope-with-the-fear-of-failure/?sh=cf2dcbc34dfc.

Clark, Nancy. "Act Now to Shrink the Confidence Gap." *Forbes*, 28 April 2014, https://www.forbes.com/sites/womensmedia/2014/04/28/act-now-to-shrink-the-confidence-gap/?sh=375e079e5c41.

Chapter 23

Hatmaker, Jen. *Fierce, Free and Full of Fire: The Guide to Being Glorious You*. Nelson Books, 2020, p. 29.

Chapter 24

Casabianca, Sandra. "Mourning and the 5 Stages of Grief."
    Psych Central, 11 Feb. 2021, https://psychcentral.com/lib/
    the-5-stages-of-loss-and-grief#denial.

Chapter 25

Shuman, Carla. "How to Cope with Change." *Psychology Today*,
    13 Jan. 2023, https://www.psychologytoday.com/us/blog/
    from-trial-to-triumph/202301/how-to-cope-with-change.

Chapter 26

McKinsey & Company. "Women in the Workplace Study."
    https://womenintheworkplace.com/.

Friedman, Ann. "What Comes After Ambition." *Elle*, 18 Aug.
    2022, https://www.elle.com/life-love/opinions-features/
    a40835443/women-rejecting-traditional-ambition-2022/.

Tsabary, Shefali. *A Radical Awakening*. Harper Collins, 2021,
    p. 286.

Chapter 28

Resource: https://www.youtube.com/watch?v=SqGRnlXplx0.

Chapter 29

Doyle, Glennon, et al. "How to Heal with Alex Elle (No. 149)."
    We Can Do Hard Things with Glennon Doyle, 9 Nov. 2022,
    https://podcasts.apple.com/us/podcast/how-to-heal-with-alex-
    elle/id1564530722?i=1000585717361. [Audio podcast
    episode].

Jennifer Thompson is a born-and-raised Central Illinoian wife, mother, writer, and marketing professional who is passionate about empowering women to live authentically. Creator of global motherhood lifestyle blog, *They Whine, so I Wine*, she possesses a unique ability to express the things many women think, but may be afraid to say. Through her raw, inspirational truth telling, tough love, and relatable humor, she's helped countless women break free of societal ideals to find joy and self-acceptance on the other side.

With an online community of over a quarter of a million women, her words have been shared and featured by international media outlets, including *Good Morning America*, *ABC News*, Yahoo.com, *The Today Show*, and KidSpot AU.

Follow her at: www.theywhinesoiwine.com or connect on social for the latest.